SELLING OPTIONS
FOR INCOME
VOLUME II

Defensive Trading,
Drawdown Management,
and Long-Term Survival

TONY PEREZ

DRAGON
PUBLISHING

Disclaimer

This book is provided for educational and informational purposes only and does not constitute financial, investment, legal, or tax advice. The material presented reflects the author's personal opinions and trading experiences and should not be interpreted as a recommendation to buy, sell, or hold any security or financial instrument.

Trading options involves substantial risk and may not be suitable for all investors. Readers should carefully consider their financial situation and consult a qualified financial professional before making any investment decisions.

Past performance does not guarantee future results. All examples are provided for illustrative purposes only. The author assumes no responsibility for any financial losses or damages resulting from the use or misuse of the information contained in this book.

Examples of trades, positions, or strategies discussed are not recommendations and are intended solely to demonstrate concepts related to risk management, defensive trading, and income strategy execution.

TABLE OF CONTENTS

THE OPTIONS INCOME SERIES BY TONY PEREZ

The Options Income Series is a practical, experience-driven guide for traders who want to generate consistent income through option selling while managing risk across all market conditions.

Rather than chasing predictions, hype, or short-term market moves, this series focuses on probability, discipline, and repeatable systems that treat trading like a business.

Each volume builds on the last while remaining fully stand-alone.

Volume I focuses on the foundations of income-based options trading, including the Wheel Strategy, cash-secured puts, covered calls, and disciplined position management.

Future volumes address capital preservation, recovery strategies, and long-term survival during volatile and declining markets.

This series is written for traders who value consistency over excitement, structure over speculation, and long-term durability over short-term thrills.

INTRODUCTION

If Volume I taught you how to generate income, Volume II is about how to survive, adapt, and grow when the market stops cooperating.

Because eventually, it will.

You may recognize where you are right now. Maybe income has slowed after months of consistency. Maybe positions that once felt manageable are now testing your patience. Maybe you've opened your account wondering whether you should adjust, wait, roll, or step aside entirely. If so, you are exactly where this book begins.

Every options seller, no matter how disciplined, will experience drawdowns, volatility spikes, positions that move sharply against them, and stretches where income slows or disappears entirely. There will be moments when emotion tempts you to abandon your system, second-guess your rules, or force trades simply to feel back in control.

This is where most traders fail, not because they don't understand options but because they were never taught how to operate defensively when conditions change.

Volume II exists for one reason: to show how professional option sellers protect capital, manage stress, and recover without panic when trades move against them.

This book assumes you already understand how to sell cash-secured puts, covered calls, and how the Wheel Strategy functions. The fundamentals are not repeated here. Instead, this volume focuses on what happens after things go wrong, when positions turn red, volatility expands, and markets test both discipline and patience.

You will learn how experienced income traders think during drawdowns, how losses are slowed without freezing decision-making, how rolls are executed with intention instead of fear, and how difficult market phases are navigated without damaging long-term capital.

Above all, this volume is about longevity, because in income trading, the trader who survives the longest is the one who ultimately wins.

Part I

WHEN THE MARKET FIGHTS BACK

The concepts in this book were not developed during ideal market conditions.

They were shaped during drawdowns, volatility expansions, assignments that didn't immediately recover, and positions that required months of management rather than days of adjustment. Many of the examples throughout this volume come from real positions managed across both Roth IRA and individual trading accounts. Some recovered quickly. Others required extended repair. A few are still ongoing at the time of writing.

That is intentional.

This book does not present perfect trades or hindsight decisions. Markets rarely cooperate that cleanly in real time. Instead, these chapters reflect how income trading actually unfolds through uncertainty, patience, and structured decision-making when outcomes are not yet known.

You will notice certain tickers appear more than once throughout the book. That repetition reflects reality, not preference. Professional traders manage positions over time, not in isolated snapshots.

The goal of Volume II is not to demonstrate flawless execution. It is to demonstrate durability, because long-term income trading is not defined by avoiding difficult periods, but by surviving them without permanent capital damage.

CHAPTER 1

WHY INCOME STRATEGIES FAIL (AND HOW PROS SURVIVE)

Most options income strategies do not fail because they are bad strategies. They fail because traders are unprepared for what happens when markets stop cooperating.

The Wheel Strategy works. Selling options for income works. Premium selling works. But only when the trader understands one critical truth: Income strategies are not immune to pressure. They are designed to function *through* pressure.

This chapter addresses the truth most trading books avoid—the period when trades stop feeling easy, income slows, positions turn uncomfortable, and confidence begins to erode. These moments are not rare events. They are inevitable phases of every income trader's career.

What determines survival is not strategy selection. It is expectation management.

1. The Myth of "Safe" Income

Many traders discover income strategies after experiencing losses from directional trading. Compared to buying options or chasing momentum, premium selling appears calmer, smoother, and more predictable. Charts move less dramatically. Premium arrives consistently. Trades appear structured.

It feels safer. Traders begin telling themselves:

- "This is safer than buying options."
- "This works in all markets."
- "If I just follow the rules, I'll be fine."

For a while, those beliefs appear true. Early success reinforces confidence. Premium accumulates. Positions expire profitably. The strategy feels almost mechanical.

Until the first real test arrives.

Every income trader remembers that moment. A stock gaps down overnight. Volatility spikes unexpectedly. Several positions move red simultaneously. Rolling suddenly feels uncomfortable. Income disappears for weeks.

Nothing about the strategy changed, but everything about the emotional experience did.

This is where most traders fail. The strategy didn't stop working, but reality violated their expectations.

Income trading was never designed to eliminate discomfort. It was designed to be managed intelligently.

2. Income Strategies Fail When Traders Expect Perfection

New traders rarely say they expect perfection, but their behavior reveals it.

- They expect income every week.
- They expect rolls to remain easy.
- They expect assignment to be avoidable.
- They expect red positions to resolve quickly.

When those expectations break, confidence breaks with them. However, professionals understand something fundamentally different.

- Drawdowns are normal.
- Slow income periods are normal.
- Repairs are normal.
- Extended management phases are normal.

Income trading is not about avoiding stress. It is about responding correctly when stress appears. The strategy rarely fails under pressure. The trader's reaction does.

Nugget: Income Strategies Don't Break—Traders Do

If a strategy works in calm markets but collapses under stress, the problem isn't the structure. It's the reaction.

3. The Real Reasons Income Traders Blow Up

Accounts rarely collapse because of market movement alone. Instead, failure tends to follow predictable behavioral patterns:

1. Oversizing positions
2. Chasing premium instead of probability
3. Panicking during volatility expansion
4. Refusing assignment
5. Abandoning rules under emotional stress

Notice what is missing from that list. Strategy failure.

The market applies pressure to every participant equally. Some traders absorb it. Others amplify it through decision-making. The difference is behavioral discipline.

Pressure reveals structure, and pressure reveals psychology.

4. A First Test Most Income Traders Remember

Early in my options-selling journey, I encountered my first genuine stress event. At the time, I did not yet understand how to use cash-secured puts as controlled entries. Instead, I purchased shares outright so I could immediately sell covered calls. I bought several hundred shares of NVDA and sold three weekly covered call contracts at a $145 strike, collecting $465 in premium.

At entry, the trade felt logical. Then NVDA began falling. News broke that China was investigating NVIDIA over potential anti-monopoly concerns. The stock dropped 3%. Then four. Then five.

For the first time, I experienced real pressure. I wasn't worried about the calls. I was worried about the shares because I entered at market price without a cushion. I suddenly felt exposed, and I remember realizing I might be trapped in a declining position without a clear defensive plan. My attention narrowed. My confidence faded. Every price movement felt personal.

What ultimately saved the trade wasn't skill. It was the underlying company. Because it was NVDA, the stock stabilized weeks later and eventually recovered, returning the position to profit.

The outcome looked successful, but the lesson was uncomfortable.

I survived because the stock recovered, not because I managed risk professionally.

That wasn't strategy. That was luck.

Volume II exists so survival does not depend on luck.

5. Professionals Trade for Survival First

Professional option sellers think differently from the beginning. Their primary objective is not maximizing income. It is remaining operational.

Before entering positions, professionals ask:

- Can I manage this if price moves further against me?
- Does this size allow flexibility?
- Am I trading large enough that I *need* success?

If success is required, risk is already excessive. Survival-first thinking slows aggression. It prioritizes adaptability over excitement and flexibility over short-term income.

That mindset protects accounts during inevitable stress periods.

6. Why Survival Creates Long-Term Income

Here lies one of trading's greatest paradoxes:

Traders who chase income directly often lose money while traders who focus on survival generate income consistently.

Why?

Because survival creates time. Time allows rolling. Time allows adjustment. Time allows volatility to normalize. Time allows probability to work.

Time is the true hedge available to option sellers. Without time, no adjustment works.

Nugget: Time Is the Ultimate Hedge

If you have time, you can roll.

If you can roll, you can recover.

If you can recover, you stay in the game.

In This Chapter, You Learned:

- Why income strategies fail due to expectations rather than structure
- Why premium selling does not eliminate market pressure
- How discomfort is a normal phase of income trading
- Why behavioral reactions—not strategies—cause most losses
- The role expectation management plays in long-term survival
- Why professionals prioritize survivability before income
- How time functions as the true edge of option sellers
- Why Volume II focuses on durability during difficult market conditions

CHAPTER 2

DRAWDOWNS WITHOUT PANIC

Drawdowns are not a sign of failure. They are not evidence that your strategy has stopped working. They are not proof that you made a catastrophic mistake.

They are a normal cost of doing business. Every trader experiences them. Every professional plans for them. Every durable income strategy assumes they will occur.

The difference between amateurs and professionals is not whether drawdowns happen. It is how they respond when they do.

Most traders panic because they never expected resistance. They entered income trading believing consistency meant smoothness. When markets push back, confidence disappears.

Professionals expect resistance, and because they expect it, they prepare for it.

1. What a Drawdown Really Is

A drawdown is simply your account declining temporarily from a recent high. Nothing more. It is not a blown account. It is not strategy failure. It is not an emergency. It is fluctuation.

Income strategies, especially options-selling strategies, experience periods where unrealized losses expand before probability reasserts itself. Institutional funds model drawdowns mathematically because they understand an unavoidable truth:

Consistency does not mean linear growth. Even the most successful funds experience periods of decline.

The objective is never elimination of drawdowns, because that goal is impossible. The objective is control. Control of depth. Control of duration. Control of decision-making while under pressure.

Nugget: Drawdowns Are the Admission Fee

If you want consistent income, drawdowns are the price of admission. The trader who can tolerate them calmly earns what others can't.

2. Why Panic Is So Dangerous for Option Sellers

Panic transforms manageable situations into permanent damage.

When traders panic, they close trades in reaction to emotional extremes. They roll defensively rather than strategically. They oversize new trades in an attempt to recover quickly. They abandon probability and begin negotiating emotionally with the market.

Options selling is fundamentally a time-based strategy. Time allows theta decay. Time allows volatility contraction. Time allows price stabilization.

Panic removes time from the equation. Once time disappears, the edge disappears. At that moment, the trader stops behaving like an option seller and starts behaving like a gambler attempting to escape discomfort.

Temporary red positions then become realized losses, not because recovery was impossible but because patience was abandoned.

3. The Professional Rule: No Decisions During Emotional Spikes

Professional traders operate under a simple but powerful rule: No major decisions during emotional spikes.

When positions move sharply against them, professionals slow down intentionally. They step away from screens if necessary. They review structure rather than react to unrealized losses.

Instead of asking, *How much am I down?*, they ask, *What is delta exposure? How much time remains? Is extrinsic value still present? Has probability materially changed?*

Most drawdowns feel urgent but are not. Markets create emotional acceleration. Headlines, price movement, and account fluctuations create the illusion that action must happen immediately.

Professionals understand that urgency is often psychological, not structural.

Nugget: Urgency Is Usually an Illusion

Markets create emotional urgency. Professionals slow down when others speed up.

4. Drawdowns Are Often Position-Sizing Problems

Many traders believe panic comes from price movement. In reality, panic usually comes from size. A properly sized position moving against you creates discomfort. An oversized position creates fear.

If a single trade causes constant account checking, interrupts sleep, dominates decision-making, or feels too important to fail, the issue is rarely the market itself. It is exposure.

The market did not create stress. Sizing did.

Proper position sizing does not eliminate drawdowns. It transforms them from crises into inconveniences, events that require management rather than emotional survival.

Example: Size-Induced Panic

After learning how to sell cash-secured puts correctly, I entered a trade selling fourteen weekly contracts on SOUN, representing 1,400 shares of exposure.

At entry, the premium looked attractive. The setup appeared logical. The trade felt efficient.

That same week, NVIDIA CEO Jensen Huang commented publicly that quantum computing remained decades away from practical implementation. The statement triggered a rapid sell-off across AI and technology-related stocks, including SOUN.

Assignment occurred at $19.50. Within days, the stock traded near $14.15. On paper, the position showed an unrealized loss exceeding $8,000.

The price movement itself was not extraordinary. Stocks move that distance regularly. The real issue was size.

The position dominated my thinking. Every tick mattered. Every headline felt threatening. I wasn't reacting to probability but to exposure.

That experience permanently reinforced an essential lesson: Drawdowns feel dangerous when position size removes flexibility.

Had the position been smaller, the same market movement would have been uncomfortable but manageable. Size determines psychology.

5. How to Respond When You're Down

When entering a drawdown, the correct first action feels counterintuitive: Do nothing immediately. Allow emotional intensity to settle.

Distance restores objectivity. Only after emotional neutrality returns should evaluation begin. Then shift from reaction to analysis:

- Is the trade structurally intact?
- Has anything fundamentally changed?
- How much time remains?
- Is meaningful extrinsic value still available?

Rolling should occur only when structure improves, not when emotions demand relief.

Professionals do not force recovery speed. They prioritize control.

Nugget: Survival Is a Strategy

You don't need to fix a drawdown quickly. You need to stay solvent long enough for probability to work.

6. The Mental Shift That Changes Everything

Most traders believe their goal is avoiding losses. Professionals understand something deeper.

You are not trying to avoid losses. You are trying to avoid irreversible losses.

Temporary red positions are expected. They are part of income generation. Permanent damage occurs only when traders panic, oversize, abandon structure, or attempt emotional revenge trading.

The amateur asks, "How do I get back to green fast?"

The professional asks, "How do I remain operational?"

That single question changes behavior, pacing, and long-term outcomes. It replaces urgency with patience, and patience restores the edge.

In This Chapter, You Learned:

- Why drawdowns are normal, not failure
- How panic destroys time-based strategies
- Why urgency is often an illusion
- How position size drives emotional stress
- A professional framework for handling drawdowns
- Why survival always comes before recovery

CHAPTER 3

BAD TRADES VS. BAD STOCKS

One of the most dangerous mistakes option sellers make during drawdowns is treating all losing positions the same. When trades turn red, emotional pressure encourages uniform responses—rolling automatically, waiting blindly, or assuming time alone will solve the problem.

But not all red positions are equal. Some trades are temporarily uncomfortable yet structurally sound. Others are tied to companies experiencing genuine deterioration, where continued patience only increases exposure. Professional traders survive because they learn to recognize the difference early, before time and capital become trapped in situations that cannot realistically recover.

Understanding this distinction changes everything about how drawdowns are managed.

1. Knowing What Can Be Fixed and What Can't

A bad trade usually reflects imperfect structure rather than a flawed underlying business. Entry timing may have been aggressive. Strikes may have been placed too close to price. Volatility may have expanded unexpectedly, or market sentiment may have shifted faster than anticipated.

Yet, the company itself remains intact. Liquidity remains strong. Institutional participation continues. The broader business thesis still exists. In these situations, discomfort comes from positioning, not ownership.

A bad stock is fundamentally different. Here, deterioration occurs beneath the surface. Fundamentals weaken. Negative developments persist. Liquidity declines. Confidence disappears. Price does not stabilize because buyers are no longer willing to support the company at prior valuations.

Bad trades can often be repaired.

Bad stocks usually cannot.

Nugget: Time Fixes Bad Trades, Not Bad Companies

If the business is broken, no amount of rolling will save you. Premium collection works best on stocks that want to survive.

2. Why New Traders Try to Fix the Wrong Things

Under pressure, traders often defend the wrong positions. Losses create psychological attachment, and admitting error feels more painful than continuing management. Stocks that have declined sharply begin to look inexpensive, reinforcing hope rather than objective evaluation.

Rolling becomes avoidance instead of strategy. Activity replaces analysis. Capital quietly becomes trapped while opportunity cost grows in the background.

Professionals approach positions differently. They attach emotion to rules, not to holdings. A position is inventory, not identity.

The objective is not proving a trade correct but preserving capital productivity.

3. How to Identify a Bad Trade That's Fixable

Repairable trades typically share several structural characteristics. The underlying remains liquid, business fundamentals remain stable, and price pressure originates from broader market movement rather than company-specific failure.

Extrinsic value continues to exist, allowing premium collection and adjustment opportunities. Time remains capable of improving probability rather than working against it.

These trades often feel uncomfortable but not hopeless. With disciplined management, time and premium gradually restore structure.

Example: A Trade That Looked Bad But Wasn't (SOUN)

After selling puts on SOUN, I was assigned 1,400 shares at $19.50 just as a market-wide shock affected AI-related stocks. A public comment regarding long-term technology timelines triggered broad selling across the sector, and the position quickly moved deeply red.

At first glance, the trade appeared broken. However, nothing fundamental about the company had changed. Liquidity remained strong, institutional participation continued, and the sell-off reflected sector-wide sentiment rather than structural deterioration.

Instead of reacting emotionally, I transitioned into covered calls. Premium collection gradually reduced effective cost basis while allowing time for stabilization. Over subsequent weeks, price action normalized and recovery followed. Eventually, covered calls were sold above the original assignment level.

This was not a bad stock. It was volatility applied to a survivable company and managed correctly.

4. How to Identify a Bad Stock That's Dangerous

Dangerous positions tend to display different warning signals. Fundamental deterioration appears repeatedly. Negative developments accumulate rather than resolve. Dilution risk increases. Liquidity weakens. Large gaps occur without meaningful recovery. Most importantly, stabilization never arrives.

These stocks punish patience. They punish rolling. They punish optimism.

Time, which normally assists income traders, becomes an adversary instead of an ally.

Example: A Bad Stock (BSPM)

Early in my trading journey, I entered Biostar Pharmaceuticals (BSPM). The shares appeared inexpensive, allowing large position control with relatively small capital. On the surface, the opportunity seemed attractive.

But the fundamentals were weak. Price declined steadily without stabilization. Institutional support was absent. Negative developments persisted, and recovery never materialized. Eventually, the company ceased operations entirely, producing a loss near $20,000.

This was not a bad trade structure. It was ownership in a fundamentally broken company.

No adjustment strategy could have repaired it.

Nugget: Rolling Is Not a Rescue Mission

Rolling manages probability. It does not fix poor stock selection.

5. The Professional Question That Changes Everything

When positions move red, professionals ask one question before taking action: *Is this a bad trade, or a bad stock?*

- If the answer is *bad trade*, management continues. Structure is improved. Cost basis is reduced. Time is allowed to work.
- If the answer is *bad stock*, exposure may need reduction or exit entirely.

Survival depends on recognizing which situation exists.

6. Why Accepting a Loss Can Be the Professional Move

Repair remains a powerful tool, but not at all costs. Capital trapped in deteriorating structures cannot generate income elsewhere. Continuing management simply to avoid realizing a loss often converts manageable damage into prolonged inefficiency.

Controlled exits preserve flexibility. Accepting a loss is not failure. It is adaptation.

Example: Selling a Losing Position to Create Opportunity (NBIS)

While holding 500 shares of NBIS, implied volatility gradually collapsed until weekly option premium became too small to justify continuing the position as an income trade. The position was no longer dangerous from a price perspective, but it had stopped functioning as an income engine.

Rather than forcing repairs, I allowed the shares to be called away, accepting a controlled loss of $678.30.

That decision immediately freed approximately $23,000 in capital, which was redeployed into a cash-secured put on HIMS, generating nearly $1,000 in premium.

The loss did not damage the account, but immobility would have.

Sometimes the best repair is redeployment.

Nugget: Capital Is Ammunition

Every dollar trapped in a broken stock is a dollar that cannot generate income elsewhere.

7. How This Skill Changes Everything

Once traders learn to distinguish bad trades from bad stocks, decision-making becomes clearer. Rolling becomes intentional rather than reactive. Drawdowns shorten. Emotional pressure declines because management decisions follow structure instead of hope.

You stop reacting to price movement and begin managing probability, and that shift marks the transition from participant to professional.

In This Chapter, You Learned:

- The critical difference between bad trades and bad stocks
- Why most traders try to fix the wrong problems
- How to identify trades that are repairable
- Warning signs of stocks that cannot be fixed
- When accepting a loss becomes the professional decision
- Why capital preservation always comes before emotional comfort

CHAPTER 4

VOLATILITY REGIMES

Most option sellers don't fail because they use the wrong strategy. They fail because they use the right strategy in the wrong environment.

Markets do not behave the same way all the time. They move through volatility regimes—distinct emotional environments that demand different expectations, pacing, and risk tolerance. Professionals survive because they recognize the regime before they react to it.

Early in my trading, I didn't understand this distinction. I believed consistency came from strategy selection. I searched for better entries, cleaner deltas, and higher premium opportunities, assuming improvement came from refining tactics. Experience eventually taught me something far more important: Consistency does not come from strategy but from environmental awareness.

The same strategy that performs beautifully in one regime can become dangerous in another without changing a single rule.

A volatility regime is not simply about price movement or market direction. It reflects the emotional condition of participants across the entire market and determines how price behaves under stress.

It answers deeper structural questions:

- How quickly prices move

- How predictable reactions remain
- How stable trends feel
- How much premium is being paid for risk
- How violent reversals become when sentiment shifts

Volatility regimes describe behavior rather than direction. Markets can rise during chaos and decline during calm conditions. What changes is not direction but forgiveness—how much room traders have to be imperfect.

Volatility regimes themselves are neither good nor bad. They are simply different. Different environments demand different behavior, and traders who fail to recognize regime shifts eventually trade position size, strike selection, and expectations that no longer match reality.

Nugget: Markets Change Before Traders Do

Losses often begin when behavior lags behind environment.

1. The Three Core Volatility Regimes

Most markets cycle through three primary environments, each rewarding different behavior and punishing different mistakes.

Calm / Low-Volatility Markets

In calm markets, price movement becomes controlled and orderly. Trading ranges tighten, pullbacks remain shallow, and recoveries occur quickly. Premiums are smaller, but win rates are higher, allowing weekly premium selling to feel smooth and predictable. Adjustments are rare, confidence builds easily, and income appears consistent.

These environments reward discipline and patience, but they also introduce a hidden danger. Success during calm regimes quietly reshapes behavior. Traders begin tightening strikes, increasing position size, reducing caution, and depending on weekly income consistency. Stability begins to feel permanent.

Nugget: Easy Markets Create Dangerous Confidence

Low volatility builds habits that fail the moment conditions change.

Calm markets are not normal. They are temporary.

Chaotic / High-Volatility Markets

When volatility expands, everything accelerates. Price ranges widen, overnight gaps appear more frequently, and intraday reversals increase as correlations tighten across sectors. Premium expands dramatically, attracting traders precisely when risk is rising fastest.

High volatility does not automatically create opportunity. It increases consequences. Positions sized comfortably during calm periods suddenly become sensitive to normal movement. Aggressive deltas move faster than adjustment decisions can keep pace, and weak stock selection is exposed immediately.

Mistakes that were survivable in calm markets become expensive during chaotic ones. Professionals recognize that volatility expansion demands defensive behavior rather than aggression.

Transitional Markets (The Most Dangerous)

Transitional regimes are where most accounts experience damage. Volatility begins rising or falling rapidly, and market tone shifts subtly before becoming obvious. Strategies that previously worked begin producing inconsistent results. Patterns fail, recoveries slow, and price moves extend further than expected.

Nothing appears broken, yet nothing behaves normally.

This period creates confusion because traders continue operating under assumptions formed in the prior regime. Old stability disappears before new stability forms, leaving positions exposed to an environment that no longer behaves predictably.

Most damage occurs here, not at market tops or bottoms but during transitions.

Nugget: Most Losses Happen During Transitions

Damage occurs when expectations fail to adjust as fast as conditions change.

2. The Hidden Danger: Regime Misidentification

Professionals rarely lose money because volatility changes. They lose money because they recognize the change too late.

Human psychology assumes tomorrow will resemble yesterday. After extended calm periods, traders continue selling options as though stability still exists. They unknowingly trade yesterday's environment inside today's market.

This delay, sometimes only weeks, creates outsized exposure precisely when risk expands. By the time volatility becomes obvious, positions are already structured under outdated assumptions. The strategy itself was never the problem. Awareness arrived too late.

3. Behavioral Carryover Between Regimes

One of the least discussed risks in income trading is behavioral carryover. Habits formed during calm markets migrate into unstable environments without conscious adjustment. Strike selection remains aggressive, size stays elevated, trade frequency remains high, and income expectations fail to adapt.

Success becomes the source of vulnerability.

The trader is not reckless. They are simply continuing behavior that previously worked. Professionals actively reset behavior when regimes change, assuming yesterday's success may now represent tomorrow's risk.

Nugget: Success Contains Future Risk

The habits that worked last month may cause losses next month.

4. Why Income Strategies Struggle
During Regime Shifts

Income strategies depend on time decay, mean reversion, controlled movement, and statistical predictability. Transitional regimes temporarily weaken all four assumptions at once.

Options begin moving faster than expected. Delta expands rapidly. Time decay becomes secondary to price movement. Rolling decisions grow more complex, and correlation increases across positions.

The strategy is not broken. Expectations simply require adjustment.

Example: Trading Through 2025 Regime Shifts

I manage the majority of my options portfolio within the technology sector, an area particularly sensitive to volatility transitions. During calm stretches in 2025, income generation remained consistent as weekly cash-secured puts and covered calls on stocks such as RGTI, PLTR, APLD, FIG, and SOFI produced steady results with minimal adjustment.

Then the regime shifted.

Earnings cycles, tariff discussions, geopolitical tension, and macro uncertainty triggered volatility expansion across technology stocks. Price ranges widened, overnight gaps increased, and correlations tightened across positions. Existing trades suddenly behaved differently despite unchanged fundamentals.

This is precisely why I avoid selling options when earnings fall within expiration windows. Earnings are volatility events, not income events.

As volatility expanded mid-cycle, expectations had to change immediately. Rather than forcing income, I adapted by using reserve capital to lower cost basis, reducing covered call deltas, slowing trade frequency, and accepting smaller premiums. Income slowed, but it did not stop. Even during transition, weekly income remained between $1,200 and $2,000 because structure adapted to environment.

Income trading does not reward prediction. It rewards adaptation. The trader who survives regime change remains present for the next opportunity.

5. Early Warning Signs of Regime Change

Professionals watch for subtle signals before volatility becomes obvious: widening daily trading ranges, increasing overnight gaps, failed breakouts, faster reversals, rising sector correlation, and headlines driving price more than fundamentals.

These signals rarely appear simultaneously, but together they indicate environmental change. Recognizing transition early allows exposure to be reduced before emotional pressure develops.

Nugget: Regime Changes Whisper Before They Roar

Volatility regimes rarely change without warning. Subtle signals appear first—wider ranges, failed breakouts, and fatter reversals—long before volatility becomes obvious.

6. The Professional Adjustment: Slow Everything Down

Professionals do not fight volatility regimes. They slow the system.

When volatility increases, position size is reduced, strikes move further out of the money, duration may be extended, income expectations decline, and flexibility becomes the priority. When volatility contracts, exposure increases gradually, probability remains prioritized, and traders stay alert for the next transition.

Income is allowed to fluctuate. Risk is not.

Nugget: Income Is Variable—Risk Is Not

Professionals allow income to change. They never allow risk to explode.

7. Stop Comparing Weeks

One of the most destructive habits income traders develop is comparing current performance to past easy weeks. That comparison leads traders to force trades, sell aggressive strikes, oversize exposure, and ignore regime context entirely.

Professionals do not compare week-to-week profit and loss. They compare risk to risk, probability to probability, and structure to structure. Consistency comes from alignment with environment, not replication of past income.

8. The Regime Awareness Checklist

Before entering any trade, professionals ask:

- Is volatility expanding or contracting?
- Is this calm, chaotic, or transitional?
- Am I sized appropriately for this regime?
- Can I manage this position if conditions worsen?

If the environment changes, behavior must change with it.

Nugget: The Market Sets the Pace—Not You

When traders force income, the market forces losses.

In This Chapter, You Learned:

- What volatility regimes actually represent
- Why strategies fail when environments change
- How calm markets create false confidence
- Why transitional markets cause the most damage
- How behavioral carryover increases risk
- Early warning signs of regime shifts
- Why adaptation matters more than prediction
- How slowing down preserves survivability
- Why traders must adjust to the market, never the reverse

Part II

DEFENSIVE TOOLS FOR OPTION SELLERS

CHAPTER 5

ROLLING UNDER PRESSURE

Rolling is one of the most misunderstood tools in options trading. Beginners often view rolling as a way to avoid being wrong. Professionals understand it differently. They see it as a method of restoring structure when a position has drifted too far from its original probability profile.

When a position moves deep in the money, emotion increases. Losses look larger. Time feels shorter. Urgency creeps in. That urgency is what destroys accounts, not the position itself.

Rolling is not a rescue mission. It is a recalibration. It is the deliberate act of improving structure under stress.

1. Why Rolling Feels Hard When It Matters Most

Rolling feels easy when the option is only slightly tested. When extrinsic value remains high, expiration is weeks away, and losses are small, rolling is almost mechanical.

It becomes psychologically difficult when delta is high, extrinsic value has collapsed, and expiration is close. That is when traders freeze or react impulsively.

The discomfort does not mean rolling is wrong. It means the position is under pressure, and pressure is exactly when discipline is required.

2. What Rolling Is Actually For

Rolling is not about avoiding assignment. In many cases, assignment is the most defensive move available.

Rolling exists to improve structure. A professional roll should accomplish at least one meaningful structural improvement:

- Lowering delta
- Adding time
- Improving break-even
- Restoring flexibility

If none of those improve, the roll is emotional instead of strategic.

Nugget: A Roll Must Improve the Position, Not Your Feelings

If a roll only reduces anxiety but worsens structure, it isn't risk management. It's avoidance.

Example: A Structural Credit Roll

Imagine selling a $30 cash-secured put with two weeks remaining until expiration. The stock declines and trades at $27, pushing the option deep in the money. Delta rises sharply and expiration pressure begins increasing.

Rather than waiting until expiration week, a professional trader evaluates structure early and rolls the position one month forward to the $28 strike for a net credit.

This adjustment accomplishes several structural improvements simultaneously:

- Additional time is introduced
- Break-even improves through collected premium
- Delta exposure decreases slightly
- Decision pressure is reduced

Nothing about the market prediction changed. The trader did not attempt to guess direction. The roll simply restored balance between time, probability, and flexibility.

The objective was not escape. It was stabilization.

Example: Rolling Under Pressure (HIMS)

In August 2025, I sold twelve cash-secured puts on HIMS at the $62 strike and collected $4,792 in premium. The stock declined, and I was assigned 1,200 shares at $62.

Then it kept dropping. Legal issues surfaced. Headlines piled up. Sentiment shifted. The stock slid lower and continued declining for months.

This is where theory ends and psychology begins. Instead of panicking or abandoning the position, I transitioned into covered calls. I focused on reducing cost basis rather than forcing recovery. I collected premium consistently, even when strikes had to be lower than I preferred.

Later, I sold additional puts at $23.50 and was assigned again, increasing total shares to 2,400.

Six months later, the adjusted cost basis had fallen to approximately $34, with over $18,700 collected in premium. The stock was trading near $16.30, still deeply below original assignment, but the position remained controlled, structured, and manageable.

Was it comfortable? No.

Was it reckless? Also no.

Rolling and premium collection were used intentionally, not to "get back to green fast," but to buy time and preserve flexibility. That distinction separates professionals from amateurs.

As of the writing of this book, I am still in repair mode on this HIMS position and new corporate developments continue to emerge around the company, reinforcing an important reality of long-duration repairs: news, sentiment, and narratives will constantly change while a position is being managed.

Professional recovery cannot depend on headlines improving. It must depend on structure.

The work is not finished, and that is exactly what professional trade management often looks like.

Repair mode does not mean failure. It means discipline under pressure.

3. Credit Rolls vs. Probability Rolls

There are generally two professional reasons to roll a position, and understanding the difference matters far more than the mechanics of the roll itself.

In some situations, a roll is executed primarily to collect additional credit and improve break-even. This approach works best when implied volatility remains elevated and meaningful extrinsic value is still available. The added premium provides incremental improvement while allowing the position more time to stabilize.

At other times, however, the objective shifts away from income and toward probability. In these cases, a trader may even accept a small debit in exchange for lowering delta, extending duration, or restoring breathing room within the position. While this can feel uncomfortable, it is not a failure. It is structural defense, prioritizing survivability over immediate income.

Nugget: Survival Comes Before Credit

The best roll is rarely the one that earns the most premium. It is the one that preserves flexibility and keeps future decisions available.

Example: A Probability Roll That Requires a Debit

Not all professional rolls produce income.

Consider a covered call originally sold at the $25 strike while shares trade near $24. Unexpected negative news pushes the stock rapidly to $18. The trader could immediately sell another aggressive short-term call for income, but doing so would severely cap recovery potential.

Instead, the trader rolls further out in time and selects a higher strike, accepting a small debit.

Emotionally, paying to adjust feels wrong.

Structurally, however, probability improves:

- Upside recovery room expands

- Assignment pressure decreases

- Future adjustment flexibility increases

Income pauses temporarily, but survivability improves.

Professionals understand that sometimes paying for time is cheaper than forcing income under poor conditions.

4. When Not to Roll

Rolling is optional, never mandatory.

There are situations where continuing to roll only delays recognition of a deeper problem. If the underlying stock is fundamentally deteriorating, if ownership no longer aligns with your portfolio plan, or if each roll increases exposure without improving structure, assignment, or even exit, may be the more professional decision.

Rolling should remain a deliberate tool, not an automatic response. Under pressure, traders often roll simply to avoid realizing a loss, believing action itself provides control. In reality, unnecessary adjustments frequently compound risk rather than reduce it.

Sometimes discipline means improving the position.

Other times, it means choosing not to act at all.

Example: Choosing Assignment Instead of Rolling

A trader sells puts on a fundamentally strong company at the $40 strike. As expiration approaches, the stock trades near $39 and extrinsic value has nearly disappeared.

Rolling forward would generate minimal credit while extending obligation another month.

Instead of rolling automatically, the trader accepts assignment. Ownership removes expiration pressure entirely. Covered calls can now be sold deliberately rather than defensively.

In this situation, rolling would have prolonged stress without improving structure. Assignment simplified the position.

Sometimes the most professional adjustment is ending the obligation rather than extending it.

5. The Emotional Trap

Most rolling mistakes are not technical errors but emotional ones.

Urgency pushes traders to roll too late, too aggressively, or simply to feel productive during discomfort. Market pressure creates the illusion that immediate action is required, when patience often produces better outcomes.

Speed rarely restores control. Structure does.

Nugget: Fast Fixes Create Long-Term Damage

If you feel rushed, you are reacting rather than managing.

6. Rolling as a Survival Skill

Rolling under pressure is not an act of brilliance. It is an exercise in restraint.

Professional traders accept discomfort without allowing it to dictate decisions. They reduce exposure when necessary, buy time intentionally, protect capital first, and preserve optionality for future adjustments.

Their objective is not to make every trade successful. It is to ensure the account remains functional regardless of outcome.

They understand a simple truth: Not every position must win, but the account must survive. Survival is what allows income to continue over time.

In This Chapter, You Learned:

- Why rolling feels hardest when it matters most
- What rolling is designed to accomplish
- How structural rolls differ from emotional rolls
- The difference between credit and probability rolls
- Why accepting a debit can improve survivability
- When assignment is safer than continued rolling
- How professionals decide when not to roll
- Why rolling protects durability, not ego

CHAPTER 6

WHEN TO ACCEPT ASSIGNMENT

Assignment is one of the most misunderstood moments in options trading.

For newer traders, assignment often feels like failure, proof that something went wrong. For professionals, however, assignment is frequently a planned transition rather than an unwanted outcome. Volume I introduced assignment as a natural component of the Wheel Strategy. Volume II reframes it as something more important—a decision point.

Handled correctly, assignment can reduce risk, restore emotional control, and create opportunities that rolling alone cannot provide. Owning shares is sometimes the safest, and smartest, move.

1. Assignment Is Not a Punishment

When a cash-secured put is sold, assignment is never accidental. It is part of the original agreement. The strike was chosen intentionally. The premium was accepted knowingly. Ownership was always a possible outcome.

Assignment simply means the position has changed form. Instead of carrying an obligation, you now own shares, at a price you selected, with previously collected premium already reducing your effective cost basis.

Nothing has inherently gone wrong.

The real danger is not assignment itself, but the emotional resistance traders often feel when it occurs. Seeing unrealized losses immediately after assignment can create the illusion that damage has occurred, even when the structure of the trade has actually improved.

Nugget: Assignment Is a Position Change, Not a Loss

You didn't lose money because shares were assigned. You transitioned from obligation to ownership.

2. Why Traders Fight Assignment and Lose

Many traders instinctively resist assignment because ownership feels permanent. Red numbers appear on the screen, flexibility seems reduced, and the position suddenly feels heavier than expected. Rolling begins to look like an escape route.

This mindset creates problems. Traders roll repeatedly for small debits, extend duration unnecessarily, and maintain obligations that no longer improve probability, all in an effort to avoid accepting shares they originally agreed to own. Stress increases, flexibility declines, and decision-making becomes reactive instead of deliberate.

Professionals approach the situation differently. Rather than asking how to avoid assignment, they ask a more useful question: Is assignment now the lower-risk option?

In many cases, the answer is yes.

3. When Assignment Is the Smarter Move

Assignment often becomes the more defensive choice when extrinsic value has largely disappeared and rolling no longer meaningfully improves probability. At that point, maintaining the obligation provides little advantage.

Ownership, on the other hand, can restore structure. Covered calls may offer clearer income opportunities. Decision pressure decreases. Time expands again.

Rolling keeps obligation alive. Assignment ends obligation. And ownership frequently provides something traders underestimate during stressful periods, breathing room.

Example: Wanting Assignment

There were times when I actually looked forward to being assigned.

I had cash-secured puts on PLTR, NVDA, and SOFI, stocks I understood and believed in. At that time, these were some of my favorite names to trade. I would intentionally sell puts just one dollar below the current stock price because the weekly premium was excellent. And I wasn't hoping they would stay above my strike. I was hoping they would dip just enough to assign me at 4:00 p.m. on Friday.

Why?

Because I knew these stocks had strong upside tendencies. Once assigned, I would immediately transition into selling weekly covered calls around 0.30 delta. The premium was consistently attractive, and the stocks often recovered quickly.

Assignment wasn't a problem. It was phase two.

Nothing is wrong with identifying two or three fundamentally strong companies and running them aggressively through the Wheel Strategy, provided position size is controlled and the fundamentals are intact.

That's not gambling. That's structured repetition.

4. Ownership Gives You New Tools

Once assignment occurs, the nature of the position changes, and so does the trader's toolkit. Ownership introduces flexibility that simply does not exist while managing short puts. Instead of operating under expiration pressure, the trader now has the ability to generate income through covered calls, adjust strikes gradually over time, and engineer cost basis with patience rather than urgency.

Unlike short options, shares do not expire. They do not force decisions on a specific date, and they do not demand immediate action when markets become unstable. That structural difference alone reduces psychological pressure dramatically. Assignment slows the pace of decision-making, allowing time to replace urgency.

In defensive trading, slowing the game down is often the safest move available.

5. Assignment vs. Rolling: The Real Comparison

Rolling and assignment are not opposing outcomes. They are different structural choices. Rolling keeps the original obligation active, maintains expiration pressure, and often requires precise timing to remain effective. While it can improve probability, it may also extend emotional stress if used repeatedly without structural improvement.

Assignment, by contrast, converts uncertainty into ownership. The obligation ends, flexibility increases, and income generation shifts toward covered calls rather than defensive adjustments. Urgency declines because time pressure disappears.

Neither approach is universally superior. The professional edge lies in recognizing when one structure becomes safer than the other and being willing to transition without hesitation.

Nugget: Rolling Is a Tool, Not a Rule

If you're rolling because you're afraid to own shares, you're rolling for the wrong reason.

6. The Covered Call Recovery Framework

After assignment, professionals rarely react immediately. The first step is often a pause, allowing emotion to settle before making adjustments. The company is reassessed objectively, separate from recent price movement, and covered calls are introduced conservatively rather than aggressively.

The focus shifts away from rapid recovery and toward gradual cost-basis improvement. Premium accumulates over time, pressure decreases, and flexibility returns. Recovery during this phase is rarely dramatic. Instead, it is slow, structured, and repeatable.

Covered calls transform discomfort into controlled income, allowing time, rather than prediction, to perform most of the recovery work.

7. Assignment and Capital Preservation

Ironically, attempting to avoid assignment at all costs often increases overall risk. Traders who resist ownership may continue rolling positions long after probability has deteriorated, trapping capital and accepting progressively weaker structures simply to delay an outcome they originally agreed to.

Accepting assignment can restore control. Ownership removes constant expiration pressure and allows decisions to be made calmly instead of defensively. Professionals protect capital not by being clever, but by choosing stability when stability becomes available.

Nugget: Slowing Down Is a Defensive Skill

Fast decisions feel productive. Slow decisions preserve capital.

8. Assignment as Strategy, Not Survival

Assignment can function as a reset, a transition point, or a structured method of restoring control when probability shifts. Used correctly, it allows income generation to continue without forcing trades or escalating risk.

The objective is not to avoid assignment forever. The objective is to use assignment deliberately, choosing ownership when it improves survivability, flexibility, and long-term probability.

In This Chapter, You Learned:

- Why assignment is not failure
- Why resisting assignment can increase risk
- When assignment is safer than rolling
- How ownership restores control
- How covered calls become income engines
- Why slowing down protects capital

CHAPTER 7

DEFENSIVE DELTA MANAGEMENT

Most traders think risk is binary. A position is either open or closed, profitable or losing, right or wrong. Professionals understand that risk rarely works that way. Exposure exists on a spectrum, and it can be adjusted gradually without panic, forced exits, or abandoning positions that remain structurally sound.

Delta is the tool that makes this possible.

This chapter is not about memorizing option Greeks or performing complex calculations. It is about understanding delta as a practical control mechanism, a defensive dial that allows exposure to be increased or reduced as market conditions change. Skilled income traders do not wait until positions become unbearable. They shape risk early, quietly, and intentionally.

1. What Delta Really Means

In practical trading terms, delta represents how sensitive a position is to price movement in the underlying stock. As delta increases, directional exposure grows. Profit and loss begin moving faster, swings feel larger, and emotional pressure rises alongside market volatility.

Lower delta has the opposite effect. Price movement matters less. Positions gain breathing room. Time regains influence, allowing probability and premium decay to work as intended.

Professional option sellers rarely obsess over precise delta calculations in real time. Instead, they develop awareness. They recognize when exposure begins to feel heavy, when positions react too quickly to normal market movement, and when emotional pressure starts increasing alongside price volatility.

That awareness becomes the signal to adjust, long before panic appears.

Nugget: You Don't Need Zero Risk—You Need Manageable Risk

The objective is not eliminating delta. It is keeping exposure small enough that clear thinking remains possible.

2. When Markets Turn Hostile

Delta management becomes most important when market conditions deteriorate. During volatile environments, price moves accelerate, correlations tighten, and multiple positions often come under pressure simultaneously. Moves that once felt routine suddenly feel amplified, not because the strategy changed, but because exposure increased relative to the environment.

At this stage, professional traders shift mindset. The question is no longer how to maximize income or capture premium efficiently. Instead, the focus turns defensive:

How can exposure be reduced without abandoning structure?

Rather than closing positions impulsively, professionals make measured adjustments that slow portfolio sensitivity. They widen strikes, extend duration, reduce position size, or accept smaller premiums in exchange for stability. The goal is not perfection.

The goal is restoring control while allowing existing trades the time needed to recover.

Example: Reducing Delta Without Closing the Trade

Assume a trader owns shares assigned at $40 and has been consistently selling covered calls near the .30 delta range while the stock trades between $38 and $42. Under stable conditions, this produces efficient income.

Then volatility expands and the stock begins moving sharply between $34 and $39 within days. Instead of continuing to sell .30 delta calls, the trader shifts defensively to the .15–.20 delta range.

Premium immediately decreases. But exposure changes dramatically:

- Probability of assignment falls
- Upside recovery room increases
- Emotional pressure declines
- Decision urgency disappears

Nothing was closed. No loss was realized. The position simply became easier to manage.

This is defensive delta management in action, reducing sensitivity without abandoning structure.

Example: HIMS in Repair Mode

HIMS provides a real-time example of defensive delta management in practice. After assignment at significantly higher prices, the stock continued declining, leaving me managing a large share position well below my adjusted cost basis.

In that environment, continuing to sell aggressive covered calls no longer made sense. High-delta calls would have increased short-term premium, but they also introduced the risk of having shares called away below my adjusted cost basis, effectively locking in losses during an already stressed phase of the trade.

Instead of prioritizing income, I shifted priorities toward control.

Under normal market conditions, I often sell covered calls near the .30 delta range. During repair mode, however, I deliberately reduced exposure by selling calls closer to the .15–.20 delta range. A .15 delta implies roughly an 85% probability of expiring out of the money, while a .20 delta suggests about an 80% probability.

That adjustment allowed premium collection to continue while significantly reducing the chance of losing shares prematurely. The objective was not optimism or hope. It was probability management. Lower delta bought time, stabilized exposure, and allowed the recovery process to remain controlled rather than reactive.

As of the writing of this book, the HIMS position remains in repair mode. Premium collection continues, exposure is managed carefully, and progress is measured gradually instead of forced.

This is what defensive delta management looks like in reality, not dramatic or exciting but structurally sound.

3. The Most Common Delta Mistake

Delta problems rarely appear suddenly. More often, they develop quietly over time. Positions drift closer to the money, volatility expands, assignments increase exposure, or initial sizing proves more aggressive than expected.

Gradually, sensitivity to price movement increases until every market move feels amplified. At that point, normal fluctuations begin to feel personal. Small price changes trigger emotional reactions, and adjustments suddenly feel urgent.

What appears to be market chaos is often simply excessive directional exposure. The environment has not necessarily become unmanageable. The position's delta has.

4. Structural Ways to Lower Delta

Professional traders reduce delta through structural adjustments rather than emotional reactions. Exposure can be moderated by:

- Rolling positions to safer strikes
- Extending duration
- Accepting assignment

- Selling lower-delta covered calls
- Reducing new trade size
- Slowing trade frequency

None of these actions abandon strategy. They rebalance exposure so the strategy can continue functioning under changing market conditions.

Example: Adjusting Cash-Secured Put Exposure

A trader normally sells weekly puts near the .30 delta on a technology stock trading at $25. During calm markets, this produces consistent premium with manageable assignment risk.

When volatility expands and daily price swings double, maintaining the same delta effectively increases directional exposure. Rather than stopping trading entirely, the trader adapts by selling puts closer to the .15 - .20 delta range.

Income slows, but probability improves significantly. If assignment occurs, shares are acquired at safer levels relative to current volatility conditions.

Professionals rarely eliminate exposure. They resize it to match the environment.

Nugget: Lower Delta Buys You Thinking Time

Time to think is often more valuable than perfect entries. Defensive delta management creates that time.

5. Assignment as Delta Control

One overlooked reality is that assignment itself often stabilizes delta exposure. Short puts near the money accelerate rapidly as expiration approaches, carrying both directional sensitivity and gamma risk.

Shares behave differently. They move linearly. They carry no expiration deadline. They remove constant timing pressure.

For this reason, assignment frequently becomes part of professional defense rather than something to avoid. When markets become hostile, slower decision environments are safer ones.

6. Delta and Position Size Are Linked

Delta challenges are frequently symptoms of position sizing rather than technical mismanagement. When a position dominates attention, controls emotional responses, or feels too large to adjust comfortably, the issue is rarely the Greek itself. The issue is allocation.

Defensive delta management only works when position size allows flexibility.

Example: Portfolio-Level Delta Control

During broad market weakness, several technology positions begin declining simultaneously. Individually, none require immediate action. Collectively, however, portfolio delta rises sharply.

Instead of reacting trade by trade, the professional trader adjusts globally:

- New trades are opened at lower deltas
- Covered calls move further out of the money
- Trade frequency slows
- Capital deployment pauses temporarily

No dramatic exits occur, yet overall portfolio sensitivity declines. Loss volatility slows. Emotional pressure stabilizes. Decision quality improves.

Defensive delta management often happens quietly at the portfolio level rather than inside a single trade.

7. Survival, Not Optimization

This chapter is not about maximizing returns. It is about maintaining stability when conditions deteriorate.

Professional income traders accept that hostile environments may require smaller premiums, slower recoveries, and temporarily reduced income expectations.

In exchange, they gain something far more important:

- Longevity.
- Preserved capital.

- Emotional clarity.
- Strategic control.

Over time, survival compounds more reliably than brilliance ever could.

In This Chapter, You Learned:

- What delta represents in real trading terms
- Why delta exposure increases during drawdowns
- How professionals reduce exposure without closing trades
- How covered call delta selection controls recovery risk
- How CSP strike selection adapts to volatility regimes
- Why assignment can stabilize portfolio sensitivity
- How portfolio-level delta management works
- Why defensive delta control protects long-term survivability

CHAPTER 8

CAPITAL ALLOCATION AS A DEFENSE WEAPON

Most traders believe capital allocation is about maximizing returns. Professionals understand that it is fundamentally about survival. How capital is deployed determines flexibility, emotional stability under pressure, and whether drawdowns remain manageable or become catastrophic. Capital allocation is not merely a mathematical exercise—it is a defensive philosophy.

Many income traders quietly adopt the belief that money not actively invested is money being wasted. That mindset destroys more accounts than bad stock selection ever will. Being fully invested removes flexibility, forces poor decisions during stress, magnifies normal volatility, and converts routine market movement into emotional pressure.

Professionals do not measure success by utilization rates. They measure it by control.

Idle capital is not wasted capital. It is insurance.

Nugget: Cash Is Not a Drag—It's Optionality

Cash creates choices. A lack of cash forces reactions.

1. The Discipline of Keeping Reserves

Every dollar deployed increases exposure while simultaneously reducing flexibility. When too much capital is committed, rolling becomes harder, assignment begins to feel threatening, patience disappears, and decision-making becomes emotional rather than structural.

Professionals allocate capital so that:

- No single trade dominates the portfolio
- No single week determines outcomes
- No individual mistake becomes fatal

Allocation is how discomfort is prevented from becoming danger.

Over time, I learned that reserve capital is not optional. I now consistently maintain roughly 20–25% of my portfolio in cash. That reserve has protected my account more effectively than any clever trade ever has.

There have been multiple situations where that liquidity allowed me to:

- Roll positions strategically
- Pay small debits to improve structure
- Lower cost basis on assigned shares
- Reduce delta during volatility spikes

In several cases, I paid for rolls rather than collecting premium because allowing assignment or forced exits would have created far greater damage.

Without available cash, those defensive decisions simply would not have existed.

Cash did not eliminate problems. It allowed them to be managed intelligently.

Example: Cash as Defensive Flexibility

Assume a trader deploys 95% of available capital selling cash-secured puts across multiple technology stocks. A volatility spike hits. Three positions move simultaneously toward assignment.

Without reserves, the trader now faces forced choices:

- Accept oversized assignments
- Close trades at losses
- Roll into poor pricing conditions

Now consider the same portfolio holding 25% cash. The trader can selectively roll only the highest-risk position, accept assignment comfortably on another, and wait patiently on the rest.

Same market. Completely different outcome.

Cash did not generate income that week, but it prevented structural damage.

2. Capital Mobility: When a "Working" Trade Isn't Working

A position does not need to be losing money to become dangerous. Sometimes risk appears in the form of stagnation.

I experienced this with NBIS while holding 500 shares and selling covered calls. Over time, implied volatility collapsed and premiums dried up. The position stopped functioning as an income engine.

The threat was no longer price movement. It was trapped capital producing minimal return.

Rather than forcing repairs or holding the shares out of pride, I allowed them to be called away in the money, accepting a controlled loss of $678.30.

That decision immediately freed approximately $23,000 in capital, which I redeployed into a cash-secured put on RGTI generating nearly $1,000 in premium.

The outcome was simple:

- Small controlled loss
- Capital restored
- Income efficiency improved

That is capital mobility in practice.

Nugget: Capital Is Ammunition

If capital is trapped in the wrong position, it cannot work for you.

Example: Opportunity Cost in Real Time

Two traders hold identical stagnant positions producing $40 weekly premium.

One exits, realizes a small loss, and redeploys capital into higher-IV opportunities producing $300–$500 weekly income.

The other waits months trying to recover emotionally.

The difference is not strategy. It is allocation discipline.

3. The Tax Reality Most Option Sellers Ignore

Another layer of allocation many traders overlook is taxation.

Premium generated inside taxable accounts creates real liabilities, even if profits remain invested. Traders often reinvest income aggressively without reserving funds for taxes, only to discover later that gains created obligations requiring liquidity.

This leads to one of the most damaging mistakes income traders make: Selling positions at unfavorable moments simply to pay taxes.

I run options strategies across two accounts:

- A Roth IRA, where income compounds tax-advantaged
- A taxable individual account, where planning becomes essential

Part of my allocation philosophy includes maintaining liquidity specifically to meet tax obligations without disturbing active positions.

Cash is not only reserved for rolling trades. It is reserved for reality.

4. Understanding Losses as Structural Tools

Professional traders also understand something many newer traders overlook: A realized loss is not always purely negative.

In taxable accounts, realized losses can offset realized gains, reducing overall taxable income generated through premium selling or capital appreciation.

For example:

If an options trader generates $25,000 in premium income during a year but realizes $5,000 in controlled trading losses through redeployment decisions, taxable exposure may effectively fall to $20,000 depending on jurisdiction and circumstances.

The loss still exists, but it improves after-tax efficiency.

This does *not* mean losses should be sought or justified casually. Instead, it reinforces an important professional mindset: Sometimes accepting a small, controlled loss improves both capital efficiency *and* tax efficiency simultaneously.

Professionals think in after-tax returns, not emotional wins.

(Always consult a qualified tax professional regarding individual circumstances.)

Nugget: After-Tax Survival Matters More Than Pre-Tax Pride

5. Allocation Must Adapt to Volatility

Capital deployment should expand and contract alongside market conditions.

During calm environments, allocation can increase moderately because risk behaves predictably.

When volatility expands, professionals slow down:

- Position sizes shrink
- Trade frequency declines
- Premium expectations fall
- Cash balances rise

Attempting to maintain peak income during hostile markets is one of the fastest ways traders overextend themselves.

Nugget: Recovery Requires Less Risk - Not More

When you are under pressure, aggression delays recovery. Stability restores it.

One of the most dangerous instincts during drawdowns is increasing size to recover losses quickly.

Professionals do the opposite. When stress rises, exposure decreases.

6. Allocation Is Ultimately an Identity Decision

Capital allocation is not just a spreadsheet calculation. It reflects how a trader thinks about survival.

The real questions become personal:

- Do I need every trade to work?
- Can I sit through discomfort calmly?
- Am I allocating capital like someone focused on longevity?

If every position must succeed for the account to remain stable, allocation is already too aggressive.

Long-term success does not require perfection. It requires avoiding catastrophe.

Small, consistent gains compound quietly over time, while large losses permanently interrupt that process.

Capital allocation determines which path a trader ultimately follows.

In This Chapter, You Learned:

- Why cash functions as a strategic defensive asset
- How maintaining 20–25% reserves preserves flexibility
- How capital mobility restores income efficiency
- Why opportunity cost matters as much as P/L
- How realized losses can improve allocation efficiency
- Why tax planning must be part of allocation decisions
- How allocation should adapt across volatility regimes
- Why recovery begins with restraint
- Why survival compounds more reliably than aggression

Part III

CONTROLLED RECOVERY & REPAIR

The most difficult period for income traders is not the initial trade, but the recovery phase that follows adverse movement. Positions drift away from ideal structure, volatility changes, and emotional pressure increases.

This section focuses on controlled recovery—how experienced traders repair positions methodically, manage drawdowns, and restore stability without allowing risk to spiral. The goal is not perfection, but disciplined repair that preserves long-term capital and keeps the income engine functioning.

CHAPTER 9

REPAIRING RED POSITIONS

Red positions are not emergencies. They are management problems.

Most traders treat red positions like fires that must be extinguished immediately. Professionals treat them more like injuries—situations requiring patience, structure, and controlled decision-making rather than urgency. The difference between long-term success and failure in income trading is rarely intelligence or strategy selection. It is discipline under discomfort.

This chapter explains how professional traders repair positions deliberately, without panic, without heroics, and without transforming temporary damage into permanent loss.

1. The First Rule of Repair: Stop Making It Worse

Before repairing anything, professionals do one thing first—they stop digging.

Most lasting damage does not occur when a position initially turns red. It occurs afterward, when traders begin reacting emotionally. They roll too aggressively, add size to recover losses, abandon probability rules, or make adjustments simply to relieve psychological pressure. In many cases, the original position remained manageable. The reaction created the real problem.

Repair begins with restraint. If the position remains structurally sound, time is still working in your favor. The immediate objective is not improvement but stabilization. Professionals understand that survival always comes before recovery, because recovery cannot occur if structure collapses first.

Nugget: Most Red Positions Don't Need Action—They Need Time

Movement creates stress. Time creates solutions.

2. What "Repair" Actually Means

Repair does not mean returning to green quickly or proving the original trade was correct. Professional repair focuses instead on restoring structure. The objective becomes improving probability, lowering effective cost basis, reducing exposure, extending decision time, and rebuilding flexibility within the position.

This shift in mindset changes everything. Professionals stabilize positions first and optimize later—if optimization even becomes necessary. Recovery becomes a process rather than an event.

3. Determining Whether a Position Is Repairable

Not every red position deserves repair. One of the most important professional skills is recognizing the difference between temporary pressure and structural deterioration.

Before acting, experienced traders step back and evaluate whether the underlying company still makes sense to own, whether extrinsic value remains available, and whether time realistically improves probability. If ownership still aligns with long-term expectations and adjustments can improve structure without increasing exposure, repair remains viable. If those conditions no longer exist, the more professional decision may eventually be exit rather than continued adjustment.

Repair begins with honesty, not mechanics.

4. The Role of Time in Repair

Time is the most powerful repair tool available to option sellers. Time allows volatility to normalize, emotional selling pressure to fade, and theta decay to continue working quietly in the background. Just as importantly, time improves decision quality by removing urgency.

Extending duration through rolling is often misunderstood as avoidance. In reality, it creates breathing room. When traders roll a challenged position forward in time, daily pressure decreases and flexibility returns. The position becomes manageable again, even if price has not yet recovered.

A common example occurs when a trader sells puts at a $30 strike and the stock declines toward $25 near expiration. Closing the trade emotionally locks in loss, but rolling forward while slightly improving strike or duration restores probability and removes immediate expiration pressure. Nothing dramatic changes overnight, yet structurally the trade becomes survivable again. Repair begins the moment urgency disappears.

A similar dynamic occurred following a sharp post-earnings drop in PLTR during 2024. Despite strong revenue, forward guidance disappointed investors and the stock declined rapidly. Nothing fundamental about the business had broken. Institutional interest remained intact, and within weeks buyers returned. The position required no prediction or aggressive adjustment. It required patience.

Nugget: Time Turns Bad Entries Into Manageable Positions

You don't need *perfect* entries. You need *survivable* ones.

5. Premium as the Second Repair Tool

During repair phases, premium collection serves a different purpose. It is no longer primarily income generation. Instead, premium becomes structural reinforcement.

Each collected credit gradually lowers cost basis, expands break-even levels, and absorbs future volatility. Professionals resist the temptation to chase large premiums during repair because aggressive strikes often reintroduce risk at precisely the wrong moment. Consistency matters far more than speed.

Consider a trader assigned shares at $40 that later decline to $32. Rather than waiting passively for recovery, conservative covered calls are sold repeatedly over time. Individual premiums may appear modest, but each cycle slowly reduces effective cost basis. Price recovery becomes less necessary because structure steadily improves underneath the position.

This approach mirrors my experience managing Micron Technology during a semiconductor downturn. The position moved temporarily underwater, yet consistent covered call sales gradually reduced exposure until shares were ultimately called away profitably. There was no dramatic rebound or perfectly timed decision—only steady structural improvement applied repeatedly.

That is what professional repair looks like.

6. Repair Happens in Stages

Professional traders rarely attempt to fix an entire position at once. Repair typically unfolds gradually. Exposure may be adjusted incrementally, time extended selectively, or only part of a position actively managed while flexibility is preserved elsewhere.

For example, a trader assigned 1,000 shares might initially sell covered calls on only half the position. This generates income while maintaining upside participation and reducing emotional pressure. As conditions stabilize, additional adjustments can be made calmly rather than reactively.

Repair succeeds because decisions remain flexible.

7. Why Speed Is the Enemy of Repair

The fastest way to destroy recovery is attempting to accelerate it. Traders often believe larger trades, tighter strikes, or aggressive adjustments will restore losses quickly. In reality, these actions usually increase fragility.

Stress appears quickly in markets. Recovery rarely does. Professionals accept incremental progress because stability matters more than speed. Structural improvement compounded over time consistently outperforms emotional attempts at rapid recovery.

8. Covered Calls as Repair Instruments

Once shares are assigned, covered calls transition from income tools into repair tools. Strike selection becomes defensive rather than aggressive. Professionals typically sell further out-of-the-money calls, prioritize probability, and accept smaller credits in exchange for maintaining control of the position.

HIMS remains a real-time example of long-duration repair. Legal developments, sentiment shifts, and regulatory concerns created extended downside pressure and multiple assignments. Rather than abandoning the position or forcing recovery, adjustments focused on stability. Covered calls were sold conservatively, reserve capital was deployed selectively, and income expectations were reduced while structure improved.

As of this writing, the repair process continues. The trade is not finished—and that reality itself illustrates the lesson. Professional repair often occurs while outcomes remain uncertain. Progress is measured not by speed but by control.

Nugget: Repair Mode ≠ Income Mode

Different objectives require different behavior.

9. Managing Expectations During Repair

Repair phases test patience more than technical ability. Income may slow, progress may feel invisible, and frustration naturally appears. Professionals normalize this experience. Instead of asking how quickly a position returns to profit, they focus on whether structure improves week by week.

If structure improves, recovery is already underway.

10. The Professional Repair Mindset

Professional repair follows a consistent philosophy. Urgency decreases. Time expands when necessary. Premium is collected conservatively. Position size is not increased simply to accelerate recovery. Capital protection remains the overriding objective.

Recovery rarely feels dramatic. It feels controlled.

Anyone can trade when conditions are easy. Professionals are revealed when conditions are not.

In This Chapter, You Learned:

- Why restraint is the first step in repair
- How professionals determine repairability
- How time functions as the primary repair tool
- How premium lowers cost basis safely
- Why repair occurs gradually rather than instantly
- How covered calls function as structural repair tools
- Why speed often destroys recovery
- How patience restores control and durability

CHAPTER 10

COVERED CALLS AS RECOVERY TOOLS

Most traders misunderstand covered calls. They often view them strictly as income generators—yield enhancers or short-term cash machines designed to produce weekly premium. Professionals see covered calls as control tools. In recovery environments, they become one of the most powerful defensive mechanisms available to an option seller.

When used deliberately, covered calls transform pressure into structure, discomfort into discipline, and damaged positions into manageable long-term opportunities. This chapter focuses on using covered calls intentionally rather than emotionally.

1. Why Covered Calls Shine After Assignment

Assignment is not failure. It represents phase two of the Wheel.

Once shares are assigned, risk becomes defined and expiration pressure disappears. Decision-making slows, urgency declines, and time begins working in the trader's favor instead of against it. Covered calls allow ownership to become productive again by gradually lowering cost basis, shaping potential exits, and generating income without introducing additional downside exposure.

This transition is where disciplined traders begin separating themselves from reactive ones. Ownership removes the ticking expiration clock that exists with short puts and replaces obligation with flexibility.

Nugget: Assignment Is a Transition—Not a Punishment

Professionals don't fear assignment. They plan for it.

2. Recovery Mode vs. Income Mode

One of the most common mistakes traders make is treating every covered call the same regardless of circumstance.

In stable conditions, covered calls may be sold aggressively to maximize income through closer strikes and rapid turnover. But when shares trade below cost basis, the position has entered recovery mode whether the trader acknowledges it or not.

Recovery mode changes the objective entirely. Instead of maximizing weekly premium, the focus shifts toward rebuilding structure. Strikes move further out of the money, probabilities increase, pacing slows, and capital protection replaces income optimization. The purpose is no longer speed. It is stability.

A trader assigned shares at $50 while the stock trades at $42 faces a fundamentally different situation than one holding profitable shares above cost basis. Selling aggressive calls near the money may produce attractive premium, but it risks locking in losses precisely when patience is required most.

Recovery trading rewards restraint.

3. Strike Selection in Recovery Mode

Strike selection becomes critically important during repair phases. Professionals prioritize distance over premium and flexibility over excitement. The key questions evolve:

- Does this strike allow room for recovery?
- Would assignment at this level be acceptable?
- Can adjustments be made easily if price rises?

Consider a trader assigned shares at $60 with the stock trading near $48. Selling a $50 covered call might produce strong premium, but assignment would permanently realize loss. Instead, selling a $58 or $60 strike generates smaller credit while preserving recovery potential.

Progress continues even if price moves slowly upward.

Nugget: A Good Covered Call Should Feel Almost Boring

If the premium feels exciting, the strike is probably too close.

4. Using Covered Calls to Engineer Cost Basis

During recovery, premium is no longer viewed primarily as income. It becomes structural reinforcement.

Each collected credit quietly lowers cost basis, improves break-even levels, strengthens resilience, and reduces psychological pressure. Professionals track adjusted cost basis rather than weekly premium totals because survivability matters more than short-term income.

For example, shares assigned at $40 may initially feel deeply underwater when price declines to $32. However, collecting $1.00 per week in conservative covered calls over several months steadily reduces effective ownership cost. Eventually, recovery requires far less price movement than originally expected.

Covered calls convert waiting into progress.

5. Time Frames That Favor Recovery

Short expirations often introduce unnecessary pressure during repair phases. Weekly calls demand constant decision-making and increase emotional fatigue when positions remain stressed.

Professionals frequently extend duration to two-to-four-week expirations during recovery. Longer duration provides smoother theta decay, stronger premium cushions, and additional time for price stabilization.

Example: Extending Duration for Better Structure

While managing AI, SOUN, and QUBT positions during periods of volatility compression, weekly premiums declined sharply while shares traded well below cost basis. Selling tight weekly calls produced minimal credit while increasing assignment risk.

By extending duration to multi-week expirations, premium improved meaningfully while strikes remained safely out of the money. The additional time reduced decision frequency and allowed underlying prices to stabilize naturally.

The adjustment did not accelerate recovery. It made recovery sustainable.

Example: Partial Covered Call Deployment

Professionals do not always sell calls against an entire share position.

Assume ownership of 1,000 assigned shares trading below cost basis. Selling covered calls on all shares immediately caps upside recovery. Instead, a trader may sell calls against only 500 shares while leaving the remainder uncovered.

This approach accomplishes several goals simultaneously:

- Income continues
- Upside participation remains
- Emotional pressure decreases
- Flexibility improves

If price rallies sharply, uncovered shares benefit fully while covered shares still generate premium income. Recovery becomes balanced rather than restrictive.

Control improves without sacrificing opportunity.

6. When *Not* to Sell Covered Calls

Sometimes the most professional decision is restraint.

Covered calls may be avoided when a stock becomes deeply oversold, when a sharp rebound appears likely, when implied volatility compresses temporarily, or when directional recovery offers greater value than immediate premium.

Covered calls cap upside. Professionals respect that trade-off.

7. Earnings Discipline: A Lesson Learned

Earlier in my Wheel trading, I occasionally sold covered calls directly into earnings announcements. The outcome was predictable—lost upside and unnecessary exposure during binary events.

Earnings are volatility events, not income events.

Today, when holding shares through earnings, I often allow the announcement to pass without selling calls. Strong post-earnings reactions frequently create better opportunities afterward, allowing calls to be sold at higher strikes with elevated implied volatility.

Skipping a trade often protects opportunity.

Nugget: Not Selling a Call Is Still a Decision

Discipline includes restraint.

8. Rolling Covered Calls During Recovery

When covered calls move in the money during repair phases, professionals focus on preserving structure rather than winning the individual trade.

Rolling early maintains extrinsic value, extends duration, and prevents emotional expiration-week decisions. The objective is not defeating the option contract but maintaining flexibility.

A trader whose $45 call moves in the money while repairing shares with a $52 cost basis may roll forward and upward, collecting small additional credit while preserving continued recovery potential.

Rolling is management, not defeat.

9. The Long Game of Covered Call Recovery

Recovery rarely feels dramatic. Progress often appears slow and uneventful. Weeks may pass with modest credits or flat performance.

Yet beneath the surface, structure improves continuously. Cost basis declines. Emotional pressure fades. Flexibility returns.

Over time, positions that once felt damaged become stable income producers again—not because of prediction or luck, but because disciplined structure allowed time to work.

Nugget: Recovery Is Invisible Until It's Complete

Most traders quit right before it works.

In This Chapter, You Learned:

- Why covered calls function as control tools during recovery
- How recovery mode changes strike selection
- How premium engineering lowers cost basis over time
- Why conservative calls outperform aggressive ones in repair phases
- How partial covered call deployment preserves flexibility
- When skipping a covered call is the correct decision
- How extending duration improves structural flexibility
- Why avoiding earnings exposure protects opportunity
- How patience transforms assignment into sustainable income

CHAPTER 11

COST BASIS ENGINEERING

Most traders think cost basis is simply a number displayed on a brokerage screen. Professionals understand cost basis is not static—it is a process.

Cost basis engineering is the deliberate and methodical reduction of structural risk over time through premium collection, patience, and probability management rather than prediction or hope. This chapter explains how experienced option sellers transform losing positions into manageable, productive ones without panic or impulsive decision-making.

1. Why Cost Basis Matters More Than P/L

Profit and loss is emotional. Cost basis is structural.

P/L fluctuates constantly with price movement, often exaggerating stress during volatility. Cost basis, however, improves through disciplined action. Professionals focus less on temporary mark-to-market losses and more on where true break-even exists, how much flexibility remains in the position, and how much room probability has to work.

As cost basis declines, options expand. Exit choices improve, probability increases, emotional pressure decreases, and control returns to the trader. Lower cost basis does not immediately change price, but it fundamentally changes risk.

Nugget: P/L Lies—Cost Basis Tells the Truth

Price can mislead. Structure does not.

2. Cost Basis Is Built, Not Fixed

There is no single adjustment that repairs a position instantly. There is no perfect roll that erases damage overnight.

Cost basis improves gradually through disciplined actions such as selling puts at stronger strikes, accepting assignment intelligently, writing conservative covered calls, rolling for structural improvement rather than emotional relief, and allowing time to work in conjunction with probability.

Recovery is incremental, and incremental progress is sustainable.

3. The Three Levers of Cost Basis Engineering

Professionals recognize that cost basis improves through only three mechanisms: collected premium, improved entry strikes, and time extension.

Every credit collected contributes to structural improvement, even when individual premiums appear small. Entering positions at stronger strikes increases margin for error, while extending duration allows probability to reassert itself.

All three levers do not need to operate simultaneously. Consistency alone produces meaningful change over time.

Example: HIMS—Engineering Structure Under Pressure

HIMS remains a live example of cost basis engineering in practice.

I initially sold twelve cash-secured puts at the $62 strike and collected $4,792 in premium before assignment of 1,200 shares. As the stock continued declining amid lawsuits, regulatory concerns, and shifting sentiment around GLP-1 treatments, I later sold additional puts at the $23.50 strike and was assigned again.

At one stage, the position appeared structurally damaged. Headlines worsened and price continued falling. Instead of exiting emotionally, I transitioned into engineering mode.

I sold repeated covered calls, selectively added exposure only at improved strikes, and focused exclusively on structural improvement rather than rapid recovery. Over time, total collected premium exceeded $18,700, lowering adjusted cost basis to approximately $34 across 2,400 shares.

As of this writing, the stock trades near $16.30 and the position remains in repair mode.

That distinction matters. Cost basis engineering does not promise instant recovery. It produces structural improvement. The position today bears little resemblance to the original assignment, not because price recovered, but because risk structure improved dramatically.

That is engineering.

Nugget: Small Credits Compound Quietly

Professionals don't chase big wins. They stack survivable ones.

Example: RGTI—Redeployment as Engineering

Cost basis engineering does not occur only within individual positions. It can also occur at the portfolio level.

After exiting NBIS and freeing approximately $23,000 in capital, I redeployed those funds into a cash-secured put on RGTI, generating nearly $1,000 in premium. That credit was more than income, it strengthened overall portfolio structure by restoring productivity, offsetting prior losses, and improving total portfolio break-even.

Sometimes engineering means repairing a position directly. Other times it means reallocating capital toward higher-probability opportunities.

Both accomplish the same objective: structural improvement.

Example: PLTR—Time as a Structural Lever

In early May 2024, PLTR declined roughly 12–15% following earnings despite strong revenue results. Guidance failed to meet elevated expectations, triggering a classic sentiment-driven sell-off.

While price action appeared severe, underlying fundamentals remained intact: GAAP profitability, strong AI positioning, and continued institutional support.

Rather than forcing adjustments, I allowed time to function as the primary repair mechanism while maintaining disciplined exposure management. Within weeks, buyers returned, and by mid-summer the stock reached new highs.

Cost basis engineering sometimes requires doing less, not more. Time itself became the lever.

4. Why Speed Is the Enemy of Recovery

The fastest way to damage cost basis is attempting to repair it quickly.

Common mistakes include selling covered calls too aggressively, oversizing repair trades, forcing premium collection, or ignoring probability in pursuit of rapid recovery. Professionals deliberately slow decision-making during repair phases.

Speed may return later. Structure must come first.

5. Cost Basis vs. Price Obsession

New traders often ask when price will return to their original entry. Professionals ask a different question: How close is break-even now?

Price remains uncontrollable. Cost basis does not. This shift transforms frustration into actionable strategy and replaces emotional waiting with measurable progress.

Nugget: Control What You Can Control

Markets move when they want. Structure moves when you act.

6. When Cost Basis Engineering Fails

Not every position deserves continued repair.

Professionals stop engineering when company fundamentals deteriorate permanently, volatility collapses beyond recovery potential, opportunity cost becomes excessive, or capital can be deployed more effectively elsewhere.

Exiting a position under those conditions is not failure. It is disciplined capital management.

7. The Patience Curve of Recovery

Recovery rarely progresses in a straight line. More often it unfolds through weeks of limited visible improvement followed by gradual structural strengthening before reaching a tipping point where pressure suddenly eases.

Most traders abandon positions during the slow middle phase. Professionals endure it.

Nugget: The Market Rewards Endurance

Those who last the longest collect what others leave behind.

8. Cost Basis Engineering Is a Skill—Not a Trick

Cost basis engineering improves with experience. It strengthens emotional discipline, stabilizes long-term income generation, and prevents catastrophic decision-making during stress.

Eventually, it becomes instinctive. Traders stop reacting to price fluctuations and begin managing structure deliberately.

That transition marks the difference between participation and professionalism, and it is how option sellers survive long enough for probability and compounding to work in their favor.

In This Chapter, You Learned:

- Why cost basis matters more than short-term P/L
- How professionals engineer recovery deliberately
- The three levers that improve structure over time
- How real positions demonstrate engineering in practice
- Why slow recovery outperforms forced recovery
- When walking away becomes the professional decision
- How patience restores flexibility and control

CHAPTER 12

SLOW RECOVERY VS. FAST RECOVERY

When a trade moves against you, every trader eventually reaches the same fork in the road. One path feels productive, decisive, and aggressive. The other feels uncomfortable, restrained, and slow. One promises immediate relief. The other demands patience.

Only one of them builds durability.

This chapter is about recognizing which path you are taking before emotion quietly makes the decision for you.

1. The Emotional Pull of Fast Recovery

Fast recovery feels logical. When traders find themselves down on a position, the instinct is to fix the problem quickly, to return to green, erase discomfort, and regain a sense of control.

That impulse is human. It is also dangerous.

Fast recovery rarely announces itself openly. Instead, it appears through subtle behavioral shifts: selling covered calls too close to the money, increasing position size to accelerate recovery, chasing larger premiums rather than higher probabilities, shortening duration instead of extending time, or entering trades designed primarily to relieve anxiety rather than improve structure.

The objective quietly changes from survival to speed.

Example: The SOUN Shock

When I sold fourteen weekly put contracts on SOUN, representing 1,400 shares, confidence was high. Then a single external comment from NVIDIA's CEO regarding quantum computing timelines triggered a rapid technology-sector sell-off.

I was assigned shares at $19.50. Within days, the stock fell to approximately $14.15, creating an unrealized loss exceeding $8,000.

The instinct in that moment was not patience. It was urgency. I could have sold aggressive covered calls immediately. I could have forced premium collection or attempted to erase losses quickly. That would have been fast recovery. Instead, I slowed everything down. I reduced pressure and transitioned into structured management rather than reactive trading.

That decision, not the stock's movement, ultimately determined the outcome.

Nugget: Speed Feels Like Control—Until It Isn't

Urgency feels productive. But urgency usually increases risk rather than reducing it.

2. What Fast Recovery Really Does

Fast recovery often delivers temporary emotional relief. Traders may even experience brief improvement or short-lived green days. Structurally, however, it usually reduces margin for error.

Speed removes time from the equation, increases fragility, and creates dependence on immediate price cooperation. Flexibility disappears, and the position becomes vulnerable to any additional adverse movement.

Fast recovery works until it fails. And when it fails, the damage is often disproportionate.

3. The Professional Choice: Slow Recovery

Slow recovery is frequently misunderstood as inactivity. In reality, it is deliberate risk management.

Rather than asking how to return to profitability quickly, professionals ask how to stabilize structure and ensure survival. They prioritize probability over premium, extend time instead of compressing it, and accept incremental improvement rather than dramatic outcomes.

Professionals willingly remain uncomfortable longer so they do not face catastrophic outcomes later.

Nugget: Professionals Trade Tomorrow First

Ask, "Will this decision still make sense if the stock moves again?"

4. Why Slow Recovery Often Wins

The paradox most traders overlook is that slow recovery often reaches safety faster than aggressive recovery, precisely because it avoids destabilizing the account.

By preserving capital, maintaining optionality, and allowing theta to work over time, slow recovery creates multiple paths back to stability. Fast recovery creates a single narrow path that must succeed immediately.

In uncertain markets, narrow paths are dangerous.

Example: MU—The Grind That Worked

MU experienced sustained downside pressure during a semiconductor sentiment shift. There was no catastrophic event, only persistent weakness.

I found myself temporarily underwater. There was no dramatic reversal or brilliant adjustment waiting to save the trade. Instead, I sold conservative covered calls week after week, collecting repeatable premium and gradually lowering cost basis. Progress was slow and often invisible, but structure improved steadily.

Eventually, I was able to exit the position profitably through a covered call assignment. There was no urgency, only disciplined execution.

That is slow recovery.

Nugget: You Can't Recover If You Don't Survive

A controlled grind consistently outperforms forced comeback attempts.

5. Executing Slow Recovery in Practice

Slow recovery is built through structural decisions rather than dramatic action. Professionals typically reduce position size, sell further out-of-the-money strikes, extend duration when necessary, favor net-credit rolls over emotional adjustments, and design covered calls for probability rather than excitement.

The objective is not to win immediately. The objective is to improve structure until winning becomes the natural outcome again.

Example: HIMS—Slow Recovery in Real Time

HIMS represents disciplined slow recovery in practice.

After assignment at $62, the stock declined sharply amid lawsuits, regulatory concerns, and negative headlines. Additional assignment later occurred at $23.50, creating an uncomfortable position on paper.

Fast recovery would have involved aggressive covered calls or increased exposure to accelerate income generation. Instead, I shifted into defensive management. Covered calls were sold in the .15–.20 delta range, premiums were intentionally smaller, reserve capital was deployed carefully, and the focus remained on lowering adjusted cost basis while preserving flexibility.

As of this writing, the position remains in repair mode.

That matters. Slow recovery is not always a finished story. Often it is disciplined management sustained over time. Structure improves first. Outcomes follow later.

Durability matters more than speed.

6. The Hidden Cost of Fast Recovery

Fast recovery frequently traps capital inside fragile structures while increasing emotional stress. Flexibility narrows, and additional adverse movement can trigger cascading risk across the portfolio.

Slow recovery does the opposite. It preserves capital mobility, reduces psychological noise, and keeps opportunities available elsewhere.

Not every dollar must be recovered immediately. Capital must remain deployable.

Nugget: Hope Is Not a Strategy

If recovery depends on perfect market cooperation, the structure is already fragile.

7. Choosing the Right Path

When facing a losing position, pause and ask these simple questions:

- Am I trying to feel better, or trade better?
- Does this decision increase margin for error?
- Can I manage the position if conditions worsen?

If the answer depends on speed, you are pursuing fast recovery. If it depends on time and structure, you are choosing slow recovery.

Professionals choose time.

In This Chapter, You Learned:

- Why fast recovery feels productive but increases fragility
- How slow recovery strengthens structure and flexibility
- Why urgency is emotional rather than strategic
- How MU illustrates disciplined grind recovery
- How HIMS demonstrates real-time professional patience
- Why survival consistently beats speed

Part IV

MARKET STRESS PLAYBOOKS

Up to this point, this book has focused primarily on individual positions. You've learned how to think clearly under pressure, manage drawdowns, roll with intention, engineer cost basis, and recover without panic when trades move against you.

But markets rarely apply stress one position at a time. There are periods when volatility expands across the entire market. Correlations rise. Multiple positions move red simultaneously. Premium behavior changes. Income slows everywhere at once. Emotional pressure compounds quickly, not because any single trade failed, but because the environment itself has shifted.

This is where traders must stop thinking in individual trades and begin thinking in systems.

Part IV exists to answer one critical question: What do professional option sellers do when the market environment itself changes?

This is the moment when most accounts fail, not from one bad decision but from unmanaged system-wide stress.

When several stocks decline together, delta compounds across positions, liquidity tightens, and decision fatigue begins to build, the rules feel different. And if your thinking does not adapt alongside the environment, small problems can compound into lasting damage.

The chapters that follow are not theoretical discussions. They are practical playbooks, repeatable decision frameworks used during real periods of market stress, including corrections, volatility expansions, earnings-heavy environments, news-driven selloffs, and portfolio-wide drawdowns.

In earlier sections, you learned how professionals repair individual positions. Here, you will learn how they prevent cascading damage before repair becomes necessary.

What Changes—and What Must Not

During market stress, many variables shift at once. Correlations increase, diversification feels weaker, premiums expand unevenly, and directional exposure compounds faster than expected. Emotional urgency rises alongside market volatility. Yet certain principles must remain unchanged.

Position-sizing discipline still governs decisions. Capital preservation remains the priority. Probability-based thinking replaces prediction, and patience becomes more valuable than activity.

Amateurs react to chaos. Professionals simplify, reduce exposure, and regain control.

The Shift From Offense to Defense

There are environments where pressing opportunity makes sense, and others where restraint becomes the edge.

Market stress demands a transition from income maximization to risk containment, from opportunity seeking to capital defense. The mistake most traders make is attempting aggressive trading in conditions that reward caution.

Markets rarely reward bravery during chaos. They reward discipline, patience, and survival.

What You Will Learn in Part IV

In this section, you will learn how professional income traders operate when pressure expands beyond a single position. You'll see how options are sold during corrections, when choosing not to trade becomes the correct decision, and how multiple stressed positions can be managed without compounding risk.

You will learn how to shift from offense to defense without freezing, how to protect income when volatility expands, and how to think at the portfolio level rather than trade by trade.

Durability is not tested during easy markets. It is tested when conditions change, and survival depends on adapting before damage compounds.

CHAPTER 13

SELLING OPTIONS DURING CORRECTIONS

Market corrections are where income traders are truly tested, not because they are rare, but because they reveal whether a strategy was built for comfort or survival.

Corrections never arrive politely. They don't send warnings or allow preparation time. They appear through sudden selloffs, broken support levels, fear-driven headlines, and correlation spikes that pull multiple positions lower at once. The real challenge is rarely the pullback itself. The challenge is whether the trader reacts emotionally or responds structurally.

This chapter examines what professional option sellers actually do when markets turn hostile.

1. A Correction Is Not a Crisis

A correction typically represents a 5 to 15% pullback affecting broad areas of the market. These moves are often driven by sentiment shifts, positioning adjustments, or changing narratives rather than permanent economic damage. Professionals expect corrections and structure their portfolios around the assumption that they will occur regularly.

Amateurs, however, are surprised by them.

Surprise creates urgency, and urgency creates mistakes. The market is not collapsing every time prices pull back. More often, it is stress-testing expectations. If a system cannot withstand a normal correction, the issue is not the market environment, it is the structure supporting the trades.

Nugget: Corrections Are Stress Tests, Not Endings

The market isn't trying to destroy you. It's testing your preparation.

2. What Changes During a Correction

When corrections begin, several structural dynamics shift simultaneously. Volatility expands, deltas accelerate, correlations tighten, and price movement becomes less predictable. Premiums rise, but risk rises even faster.

This is where many income traders become trapped. Elevated premium feels like opportunity, when in reality it is simply compensation for uncertainty. Without adjusting size or strike selection, traders are not being rewarded, they are increasing exposure.

Professionals respond by slowing the entire system down. Contract size decreases. Strike distance widens. Trade frequency drops. Income expectations are reduced deliberately. The objective shifts away from optimization and toward preservation.

3. What Does Not Change

Despite changing conditions, professionals do not abandon core principles. Probability remains central. Position-sizing discipline stays intact. Capital-preservation rules remain nonnegotiable. Emotional control becomes even more important.

The strategy itself does not change, only the tempo does.

Nugget: Corrections Don't Require New Strategies—Just Better Discipline

The rules don't change. Your patience does.

Example: The 2025–2026 Tech Correction

During repeated volatility expansions across the tech and AI sectors, my portfolio, heavily weighted toward technology, experienced simultaneous pressure across both Roth and individual accounts. This is where corrections become psychological rather than technical.

Managing one red position is manageable. Managing several at once tests conviction.

QUBT provided an important lesson. As price declined, implied volatility began compressing instead of expanding. Weekly covered calls stopped producing meaningful premium. Rather than forcing trades for minimal credit, I extended expirations two to four weeks, allowing better premium collection while maintaining safer strike distance.

Income slowed, but structure improved.

RGTI presented the opposite environment. Premium expanded dramatically, creating the temptation to increase size or sell closer strikes. Instead, contract count was reduced and strike distance widened. Reserve capital was preserved, preventing any single position from dominating portfolio exposure.

SOUN demonstrated correlation risk. The stock weakened alongside the broader AI sector despite no catastrophic company-specific news. Rather than averaging down aggressively, I focused on managing existing exposure, lowering deltas, and avoiding new risk additions.

Participation continued. Aggression stopped.

Nugget: Corrections Punish Aggression, Not Participation

You can keep trading. You just can't keep pressing.

4. The Most Dangerous Correction Mistake

The largest error traders make during corrections is attempting to maintain normal income during abnormal conditions. This leads to tighter strikes, larger positions, emotional rolling, and compounding drawdowns.

Corrections are not income-maximizing environments. They are capital-preservation environments.

Nugget: Income Can Wait—Capital Cannot

You can't sell options next month if you destroy your account this month.

5. Adjusting Without Abandoning

Professionals rarely stop trading entirely during corrections, but they become highly selective. Probability takes precedence over premium size. Assignment is accepted more calmly. Portfolio complexity is reduced. Trades are allowed more time to develop.

The objective is not to defeat the correction. It is to exit it intact.

6. Why Corrections Create Opportunity

Corrections reset expectations, compress valuations, and remove weak positioning from the market. Traders who survive difficult phases enter calmer environments with preserved capital, improved cost bases, and emotional clarity.

Those who panic often miss recovery, not because their market outlook was wrong, but because their structure failed before conditions improved.

Nugget: Corrections Reward Prepared Traders

The money is made after the correction, by those who didn't self-destruct during it.

In This Chapter, You Learned:

- Why corrections are normal market behavior
- What structurally changes during volatility expansion
- What must remain constant under pressure
- How professionals adjust without abandoning strategy
- Why elevated premium demands elevated caution
- How portfolio thinking prevents cascading mistakes
- Why survival during corrections enables future income

CHAPTER 14

EARNINGS, NEWS, AND VOLATILITY SPIKES

Most income traders do not lose money because their strategy fails. They lose money because they voluntarily accept risks that never needed to be taken. They don't avoid unnecessary damage.

Earnings announcements, unexpected headlines, and volatility spikes are not normal market environments. They are known danger zones. Professionals respect them. Amateurs trade directly into them.

This chapter focuses on avoiding unnecessary damage, not through prediction, but through exposure control.

1. Why Earnings Are Different

Earnings events compress weeks of price discovery into a single moment. Overnight gaps replace gradual movement, and probability temporarily disappears from the equation.

Before earnings, implied volatility expands and premiums appear attractive. After earnings, volatility collapses instantly, and option pricing resets. Strikes that appeared safe hours earlier can suddenly become deeply threatened.

Income strategies depend on time decay and controlled movement. Earnings remove both.

Nugget: Earnings Remove Time From the Equation

When earnings hit, probability pauses and price takes over.

2. Why Earnings Premium Feels So Attractive

Income traders are often pulled toward earnings events for a simple reason: the premium suddenly looks exceptional. Contracts that normally generate modest income begin offering unusually large credits. Probability metrics may still appear favorable, and strikes sitting comfortably out of the money can create the illusion of safety.

This creates a powerful psychological trap. The trade appears disciplined rather than speculative. The trader begins rationalizing participation. Thoughts emerge quietly: *the delta is still low, the company usually doesn't move that much*, or *just this one expiration won't matter.*

Professionals recognize this moment immediately. Elevated premium before earnings is not a reward for skill. It is compensation for uncertainty that cannot be modeled reliably. The market is transferring risk, not offering opportunity.

Earnings losses rarely occur because traders misunderstand risk. They occur because traders justify accepting risk they would normally avoid.

Nugget: Attractive Premium Often Signals Hidden Uncertainty

When payment rises suddenly, ask what risk the market is transferring to you.

3. A Lesson Learned the Hard Way

Early in my Wheel trading, I did not consistently track earnings dates. Weekly options were sold simply because premiums looked attractive. The strategy itself wasn't flawed, but the exposure was unnecessary.

Losses came not from poor execution, but from volunteering for binary risk.

Today, if earnings fall within the option's expiration window, I do not sell that contract. No exceptions. That single rule eliminated an entire category of preventable damage.

4. When Probability Suddenly Stops Working

Before earnings, option pricing still displays familiar statistics. Delta suggests high probability. Historical movement appears manageable. The trade looks no different from any other weekly position.

Then earnings arrive. A company may gap 10, 15, or even 20% overnight. The move occurs outside trading hours, eliminating the ability to adjust, roll, or reduce exposure. A position that appeared statistically safe hours earlier may open deeply in the money before any defensive action is possible.

This is the defining difference between earnings risk and normal market movement. During standard trading conditions, price typically travels through levels gradually, allowing time for decision-making. Earnings replace gradual movement with instantaneous repricing.

Probability does not fail during earnings events. It temporarily becomes irrelevant.

Professionals avoid environments where adjustment is impossible. Survival depends less on being correct and more on maintaining the ability to respond.

5. The Professional Rule on Earnings

If earnings occur before expiration, professionals wait.

This applies equally to cash-secured puts, covered calls, rolls, and adjustments. Professionals do not make exceptions based on confidence or narrative conviction. They respond after outcomes are known rather than gambling beforehand.

Waiting is not hesitation. It is risk management.

6. When Skipping Earnings Creates Opportunity

Ironically, some of the best trades occur after earnings. By skipping covered calls during earnings week, upside exposure remains intact. A strong earnings reaction often produces both higher prices and elevated implied volatility afterward.

Selling calls after the event allows traders to respond to confirmed information instead of predicting outcomes.

After earnings are released, uncertainty declines immediately. Directional reactions may still be strong, but the unknown variables that inflated option pricing have largely been resolved. Implied volatility contracts, spreads normalize, and price begins forming new ranges.

This is when probability returns.

Professionals prefer entering positions after information becomes public rather than attempting to anticipate outcomes beforehand. Waiting allows strikes to be selected using confirmed price levels instead of assumptions. Covered calls can be sold against strength, or cash-secured puts initiated after exaggerated reactions stabilize.

Patience transforms earnings from a threat into opportunity.

Nugget: Professionals Trade Reactions, Not Predictions

Information revealed is safer than information anticipated.

7. News Risk: Earnings Without a Schedule

Unlike earnings, news risk arrives without warning. Regulatory developments, geopolitical events, tariff discussions, macro commentary, analyst downgrades, or sudden corporate announcements can trigger immediate repricing events.

The danger is not news itself, it is being sized as though news cannot occur.

Modern markets process information instantly. Headlines travel faster than traders can react, and price adjustments often occur before defensive decisions are possible.

Professionals assume unknown risk always exists. Because timing cannot be predicted, exposure must remain survivable.

Nugget: Unknown Risk Is the Most Expensive Risk

If risk timing cannot be defined, reduce exposure.

8. Volatility Spikes Change the Rules

During volatility expansions, option pricing inflates, spreads widen, and directional movement accelerates. Rolling becomes more expensive and emotional pressure rises.

High implied volatility is not permission to trade aggressively. It is a signal to tighten discipline. Volatility spikes often create the illusion of opportunity because premium expands rapidly. Larger credits suggest greater income potential, encouraging traders to increase size or sell closer strikes.

At the same time, correlations across stocks begin rising. Names that normally move independently start reacting to the same macro forces. Diversification weakens precisely when traders believe they are being compensated more generously.

Multiple positions may move against the portfolio simultaneously, amplifying stress and reducing flexibility.

High volatility increases consequence as much as compensation.

During 2026 tech volatility expansions, I responded by lowering deltas, widening strikes, reducing size, and accepting slower income. The objective was containment, not maximization.

Nugget: Income Is Variable - Risk Is Not

Professionals allow income to change. They never allow risk to explode.

9. The No-Volunteer Risk Principle

Professional traders accept only risk that is defined, manageable, compensated, and optional. Earnings and surprise events frequently meet none of these conditions.

Missing a trade carries no penalty. Participating in unnecessary risk introduces asymmetric outcomes where downside greatly exceeds potential reward.

Nugget: You Don't Need Every Premium

Missing a trade costs nothing. Forcing one can cost everything.

10. What Professionals Do Instead

As major events approach, professionals allow options to expire, roll early if necessary, or sit in cash without guilt. They observe market reactions and re-enter once volatility stabilizes and structure returns.

Patience converts uncertainty into opportunity. Professionals understand that capital preserved today becomes opportunity tomorrow.

In This Chapter, You Learned:

- Why earnings create binary risk
- Why elevated premium often signals hidden uncertainty
- How probability temporarily disappears during earnings events
- Why professionals avoid environments where adjustment is impossible
- The professional rule for earnings exposure
- Why trading reactions is safer than predicting outcomes
- How unscheduled news creates hidden portfolio risk
- Why volatility spikes increase consequence as well as opportunity
- How correlation risk rises during market stress
- Why skipping trades protects long-term capital
- How exposure control prevents unnecessary damage

CHAPTER 15

WHEN MULTIPLE POSITIONS GO RED

One red position is a trade problem. Multiple red positions become a portfolio problem.

This is where many income traders struggle, not because individual trades are unmanageable, but because simultaneous stress overwhelms decision-making. Positions that were previously comfortable begin moving together. Losses appear across the screen at the same time. Confidence declines even when no single trade is catastrophic.

Professionals respond by changing perspective. They stop thinking trade by trade and begin managing the portfolio as a system.

Survival at this stage depends less on technical skill and more on understanding how portfolios behave under pressure.

1. Why Multiple Red Positions Feel Dangerous

When several positions decline together, emotional pressure rises quickly. Traders often interpret simultaneous losses as evidence that something has fundamentally gone wrong. Attention narrows. Every price movement feels urgent. Every decision feels consequential.

The psychological impact is disproportionate to the actual risk. In reality, simultaneous weakness is usually driven by correlation rather than individual failure. Market environments shift, liquidity tightens, sentiment changes, and entire sectors move together regardless of company-specific fundamentals.

During periods of technology-sector volatility in 2026, positions such as HIMS, RGTI, SOUN, and QUBT weakened simultaneously. The environment changed faster than expectations adjusted. Multiple positions turning red did not mean every thesis had failed. It meant the market regime had shifted.

Professionals recognize this moment as a known phase of trading rather than a personal mistake.

Nugget: Correlation Is Not Catastrophe

When everything turns red together, the market is speaking, not accusing.

2. The Hidden Reality of Correlation

Many traders believe diversification guarantees protection. Under normal conditions, different stocks behave independently enough to reduce overall volatility.

During stress events, however, correlations expand rapidly. Stocks that normally move differently begin reacting to the same macro forces. Interest rate expectations, geopolitical headlines, liquidity changes, or sector sentiment cause positions to move in unison. Diversification temporarily weakens precisely when protection feels most necessary.

This creates the illusion that risk has suddenly increased beyond control. In truth, correlation expansion is temporary. Markets eventually differentiate again. Professionals understand that simultaneous red positions often reflect environmental pressure rather than structural failure.

The mistake is reacting as though every position must be solved immediately.

3. The Biggest Mistake

Amateurs attempt to fix everything at once. They roll multiple positions simultaneously. They close trades emotionally. They oversize recovery trades in an attempt to accelerate improvement. They abandon probability in favor of urgency.

Activity creates the illusion of control.

Professionals instead pause and ask one critical question: What actually requires action right now?

Many red positions require nothing more than time. Acting unnecessarily often converts manageable stress into permanent damage.

4. Step One: Stop Adding Risk

When portfolio stress appears, professionals immediately slow expansion. New trades stop. Trade frequency declines. Adjustments become deliberate rather than reactive. The objective shifts from income generation to structural stability.

This pause is not fear. It is containment.

During recent volatility phases, portfolios that felt emotionally overwhelming often remained structurally survivable because cash reserves, duration, and flexibility still existed.

Stress is not collapse. Recognizing that distinction prevents escalation.

5. Step Two: Assess the Portfolio—Not the Trades

Professionals evaluate exposure at the portfolio level before touching individual positions.

Key questions include:

- How concentrated is exposure within one sector?
- How much buying power remains?
- Which positions share correlated risk?
- How much time exists across expirations?
- Is assignment manageable across multiple names?

Only after answering these questions do adjustments begin so that portfolio awareness can replace emotional reaction.

6. Triage: Not All Positions Are Equal

Under pressure, professionals apply triage.

Positions typically fall into one of four categories:

1. Stable Positions – Require no action and retain sufficient time or distance.
2. Manageable Positions – May benefit from future adjustment but are not urgent.
3. Priority Positions – Require structural improvement soon.
4. Exit Candidates – Consume capital inefficiently or increase overall risk.

Energy and attention are allocated accordingly. Attempting to fix every position equally wastes both emotional and financial capital.

Nugget: Not All Red Positions Deserve Equal Energy

Attention is capital. Spend it wisely.

7. Portfolio Thinking in Practice

During simultaneous pressure across multiple technology holdings, adjustments shifted away from individual trade optimization, toward overall survivability.

New entries were reduced. Covered call deltas were lowered. Premium expectations decreased. Reserve capital was preserved rather than deployed aggressively. Income slowed temporarily. Stability improved immediately.

Portfolio-level management often feels less productive because fewer visible actions occur. Yet this restraint prevents cascading errors that typically occur during stressful environments.

Professionals manage exposure first and income second.

8. Reduce Decisions, Not Just Risk

Stress increases cognitive load. The human brain performs poorly when forced to process too many decisions simultaneously.

Professionals respond by simplifying. Oversized exposure may be trimmed. Weak positions consolidated. Expiration cycles reduced. Complexity intentionally lowered.

The objective is not optimization. The objective is clarity. Fewer decisions restore control faster than better decisions made under pressure.

Nugget: Clarity Is Defensive Capital

When stress rises, simplify before optimizing.

9. The Power of Cash

Cash stabilizes portfolios during stress by eliminating urgency.

Liquidity prevents forced adjustments, which allows selective action instead of emotional liquidation. It restores optionality, the ability to choose rather than react.

Reserve capital transforms stressful environments into manageable ones. Traders with liquidity can improve positions deliberately. Traders without it become defensive participants.

Cash is not inactivity. It is strategic flexibility.

Nugget: Cash Is a Position

During stress, liquidity becomes leverage.

10. Avoid the "Everything Must Be Fixed" Trap

Markets recover unevenly. Portfolios do too.

Some trades rebound quickly. Others stabilize slowly. A few may require exit. Professionals do not demand synchronized recovery across all positions. They accept asymmetry.

The goal is not perfection across every trade. The goal is maintaining portfolio function while recovery unfolds naturally.

Demanding immediate resolution creates unnecessary risk.

11. How Portfolio Stress Ends

Portfolio stress rarely resolves through a single adjustment or dramatic market reversal. It fades gradually as volatility contracts, correlations weaken, and exposure naturally declines through expiration and adjustment.

Professionals rebuild cautiously. Position size increases slowly. Trade frequency returns gradually. Income targets expand only after stability has clearly returned.

Recovery is not an event. It is a phase.

Nugget: Recovery Is a Phase, Not a Trade

Accounts rarely recover through one winning position. Stability returns through disciplined risk control and gradual rebuilding.

In This Chapter, You Learned:

- Why multiple red positions create psychological pressure
- How correlation expansion causes simultaneous losses
- Why diversification temporarily weakens during volatility
- The professional shift from trade thinking to portfolio thinking
- Why stopping new trades stabilizes accounts
- How professionals triage portfolio exposure
- Why reducing decisions restores control
- How cash provides strategic flexibility
- Why not all positions require action
- How portfolio recovery unfolds gradually rather than instantly

PART V

THE PROFESSIONAL TRADER'S SURVIVAL MINDSET

Income trading is not sustained by strategy alone. Long-term survival depends on discipline, patience, and the ability to think beyond individual trades. Markets change, volatility expands and contracts, and emotional pressure rises during difficult periods.

This section focuses on the mindset required to endure those cycles. Professional traders survive not because they avoid adversity, but because they develop the psychological structure to navigate it calmly and consistently.

CHAPTER 16

EMOTIONAL CONTROL
IN DRAWDOWNS

Drawdowns rarely destroy trading accounts. Emotional reactions do.

Most traders fail during difficult periods not because their strategy stops working, but because emotions take control at the exact moment discipline matters most. This chapter focuses on mastering the internal side of trading—the part no platform, indicator, or system can manage for you.

Drawdowns attack confidence, control, and income expectations simultaneously. For income traders, this feels deeply personal. You were not gambling or speculating; you were operating a structured system designed to generate consistency. When income slows or positions move red, the brain interprets the change as danger. Fear, frustration, urgency, and self-doubt quickly follow.

I experienced this firsthand during the 2026 technology volatility cycle. Multiple positions came under pressure at once. HIMS required extended repair. RGTI moved unpredictably. SOUN and QUBT swung aggressively with market sentiment. Some weeks premiums compressed, while others brought sudden volatility spikes. Income slowed—not because the strategy failed—but because market conditions shifted.

That is precisely when emotions attempt to take control.

Professional traders do not eliminate emotion. They learn to contain it.

Nugget: Emotion Is Information—Not Instruction

Feeling stress does not mean action is required. It means awareness is required.

1. Why Drawdowns Feel So Personal

Income trading creates psychological expectations. Weekly premium becomes familiar. Expirations reinforce confidence. Accounts grow steadily.

Then suddenly, progress pauses. Premium shrinks. Positions require management instead of expiration. Adjustments replace routine income. The brain interprets this change as failure—even when nothing structurally dangerous has occurred.

One of the most difficult moments I experienced came during a stretch when several technology positions declined simultaneously. My account value fluctuated daily despite continuous premium collection. Rationally, I understood the positions were manageable. Emotionally, however, it felt as though progress had stopped.

That emotional discomfort created an impulse to act—to roll faster, sell closer strikes, or initiate new trades simply to restore income flow.

None of those actions would have improved the situation. The problem was not the trades. It was the discomfort of uncertainty.

2. The Psychological Traps of Drawdowns

During drawdowns, traders tend to fall into predictable behavioral patterns.

Action bias encourages unnecessary adjustments simply to feel productive. Revenge trading attempts to recover losses quickly. Rule drift introduces exceptions "just this once." Income obsession pressures traders into forcing weekly results. Catastrophizing transforms temporary setbacks into imagined permanent failure.

I have experienced each of these impulses personally.

During one volatile period, after several slow income weeks, I caught myself scanning positions for trades I *could* make rather than trades I *should* make.

Nothing required adjustment, yet inactivity felt uncomfortable. That discomfort alone nearly pushed me into selling aggressive short-dated options purely to recreate normal income levels.

That would have increased risk precisely when stability was needed.

Each emotional reaction converts manageable stress into lasting damage. Professionals separate feelings from decisions. They do not ask how they feel about a trade. Instead, they ask:

- Does probability remain intact?
- Is time still available?
- Is position size manageable?
- Is capital protected?

Feelings are acknowledged but never granted authority.

Nugget: Calm Is a Skill—Not a Personality Trait

Emotional control is trained through repetition under stress.

3. The 24-Hour Rule

One of the most important internal rules I follow is simple: No major decisions during emotional spikes.

When anxiety, urgency, anger, embarrassment, or desperation appear, I step away from the screen. Many of my best trading decisions were made twenty-four hours after I wanted to act.

During the 2026 volatility expansion, several positions moved sharply lower intraday. The immediate instinct was to roll aggressively or hedge exposure. Instead, I waited until the following trading session. By then, volatility had stabilized, spreads improved, and clearer adjustment opportunities appeared.

The decision improved simply because emotion faded.

Options selling is fundamentally a time-based strategy. Slower decisions often produce better outcomes. Speed benefits option buyers. Patience benefits sellers.

4. When Income Slows

One of the most dangerous thoughts an income trader can have is: *I need income this week.*

That belief quietly destroys discipline, leading to:

- tighter strikes
- higher deltas
- oversized positions
- trading through earnings
- ignoring regime conditions

Early in my trading development, I occasionally increased trade frequency during slow periods simply to maintain income consistency. Those weeks almost always introduced unnecessary stress later.

Professionals never depend on income from a specific week. Their systems are designed to function across months and years.

If one slow week creates panic, the issue is rarely strategy—it is allocation or sizing.

Nugget: Needing Income Is a Position-Sizing Problem

Fear often reveals excessive exposure.

5. Structure Regulates Emotion

Professionals rely less on willpower and more on structure.

During stressful environments, I intentionally shift behavior:

- fewer new trades
- lower deltas
- higher cash reserves
- scheduled portfolio reviews
- reduced screen time
- predefined adjustment rules

These structural safeguards absorb emotional pressure before it becomes decision damage.

During extended HIMS repair, for example, I limited portfolio adjustments to predetermined review windows rather than reacting intraday. That single rule prevented dozens of unnecessary decisions.

Structure replaces impulse.

6. Experience Changes Emotional Response

Emotional control improves through exposure.

The first major drawdown feels overwhelming. Every red day feels threatening. Every decision feels consequential.

But something changes after surviving multiple cycles. You begin recognizing familiar patterns:

- volatility expands
- income slows
- fear rises
- markets stabilize
- recovery begins

The tenth drawdown feels different from the first, not because losses disappear but because experience proves they pass.

Eventually, fear loses authority.

Nugget: Survival Creates Confidence

Confidence comes from surviving stress without permanent damage.

7. The Professional Emotional Framework

Professional traders understand a truth many never learn:

You do not need to win today. You need to remain functional tomorrow.

Drawdowns test identity more than strategy. Traders who define success by short-term outcomes experience constant emotional instability. Traders who define success by survivability maintain clarity even during stress.

Emotional control does not eliminate discomfort. It prevents discomfort from becoming destruction.

In This Chapter, You Learned

- Why drawdowns trigger powerful emotional reactions
- How income slowdown creates psychological pressure
- The behavioral traps traders fall into under stress
- Why delaying decisions improves outcomes
- How income dependency leads to poor risk decisions
- Why structure regulates emotion better than willpower
- How experience reduces emotional volatility over time
- Why survivability—not perfection—builds lasting confidence

CHAPTER 17

POSITION SIZING THAT SAVES ACCOUNTS

Most trading blowups do not occur because a trader was wrong. They occur because the trader was too large.

Position sizing quietly determines emotional stability, rolling flexibility, drawdown survivability, and long-term income consistency. A trader can operate an excellent Wheel Strategy, follow disciplined entry rules, and select fundamentally sound companies, yet improper sizing eventually overrides every other advantage.

The market can only harm an account through exposure. A 5% move in a stock is manageable when allocation is appropriate. The same move becomes emotionally overwhelming when position size is excessive. Price movement does not change. Psychological impact does.

I learned this lesson clearly with SOUN. Selling fourteen contracts—representing 1,400 shares—appeared efficient at entry. Premium looked attractive and the setup appeared logical. Then a single macro headline drove the stock sharply lower. The move itself was not extraordinary, but the size magnified its impact dramatically.

The drawdown felt severe not because the stock declined unusually, but because the position dominated both capital and attention.

The strategy had not failed. Position sizing had.

Professionals obsess over size more than entries.

Nugget: Risk Is Not the Trade—It's the Size

Even good trades become dangerous when position size is excessive. Survival is determined by exposure, not entry.

1. How Oversizing Quietly Develops

Oversizing rarely feels reckless at entry. It often develops gradually through:

- adding contracts after early success
- repeating trades in familiar tickers
- increasing size during calm markets
- reinvesting premium too aggressively
- believing consistency will continue indefinitely

Each individual decision feels reasonable. Collectively, exposure compounds.

During the 2026 technology volatility phase, heavy exposure across names like HIMS, RGTI, and QUBT revealed how correlation multiplies risk. Multiple positions weakened simultaneously, not because each company failed independently, but because sector sentiment shifted at once.

Suddenly, several manageable trades became one large portfolio problem.

Oversizing produces:

- anxiety
- tunnel vision
- emotional attachment
- shortened decision timelines
- and the psychological need for trades to succeed

Once a position feels *too large to lose*, probability analysis disappears and pain avoidance replaces rational management.

Example: When Size Removes Patience

At one point, I carried a larger-than-normal allocation in HIMS while volatility expanded unexpectedly. The position itself remained repairable, but its size increased emotional sensitivity to daily price movement.

Every dollar move felt significant. Nothing structural required immediate action, yet the temptation to adjust constantly increased. Had the position been half the size, the same price movement would have registered as routine volatility instead of psychological pressure.

That experience reinforced an important truth: Sizing determines whether time feels available.

Professionals size trades so they can:

- sleep comfortably
- wait patiently
- accept assignment calmly
- and evaluate decisions objectively

When clarity disappears, size is usually the underlying cause.

Nugget: If I'm Hoping, I'm Oversized

Hope enters trading when exposure exceeds comfort.

2. The Professional Allocation Framework

A practical guideline protects most income traders: No single Wheel position should exceed roughly 15–20% of total account value, including reserved assignment capital or owned shares.

This guideline accomplishes several defensive objectives:

- prevents one ticker from dominating outcomes
- preserves buying power during volatility
- allows rolling flexibility
- prevents forced liquidation elsewhere
- maintains emotional neutrality

As I diversified exposure across names such as PLTR, NVDA, and SOFI rather than concentrating heavily in one ticker, stress declined immediately. Nothing about the strategy changed. Only the size changed, and performance stability improved.

3. Why Smaller Positions Often Win

Smaller positions appear inefficient to newer traders because premium collected per trade decreases. But survivability increases.

When PLTR experienced a sharp post-earnings decline in 2024, manageable sizing allowed patience instead of reaction. There was no urgency to defend the position aggressively. Covered calls were sold conservatively, time passed, and the stock ultimately recovered.

That recovery was only possible because size allowed time to work.

Oversized traders rarely reach recovery. They are forced into decisions before probability can help them.

Proper sizing preserves:

- capital
- flexibility
- emotional stability
- and decision quality

4. Assignment Risk Is Really Size Risk

Assignment itself is not dangerous. Unplanned assignment *at excessive scale* is.

Professionals assume assignment will occur eventually and size positions so ownership integrates naturally within portfolio design. Shares should feel manageable, not threatening.

If assignment creates panic, the position was oversized before assignment occurred. Balanced allocation converts panic into inconvenience and urgency into optionality.

Calm is not personality. It is allocation discipline.

Nugget: Calm Is Purchased With Small Size

Calm is not a personality trait in trading. It is the result of position sizes that remain manageable during volatility.

5. Scaling the Professional Way

Professionals do not increase size after wins. They increase size only after surviving adversity.

Scaling occurs gradually:

- after navigating drawdowns
- after managing assignments successfully
- after demonstrating emotional consistency
- after proving repair discipline

Markets will always deliver surprises. Position sizing functions as the emergency brake—the one variable fully under trader control.

Aggressive sizing seeks acceleration. Professional sizing seeks endurance.

6. The Compounding Advantage of Survival

The professional survival equation is simple:

Small size + time + discipline = recovery

Remove size control, and time disappears. Remove time, and probability cannot function. Remove discipline, and recovery becomes unlikely.

Long-term income trading rewards traders who remain operational through multiple market cycles, not those who maximize short-term premium.

Nugget: Surviving Is a Form of Winning

Longevity compounds faster than aggression.

In This Chapter, You Learned

- Why position size—not prediction—determines risk
- How oversizing creates emotional decision-making
- Why correlation magnifies exposure during volatility
- The professional 15–20% allocation guideline
- How proper sizing preserves rolling flexibility
- Why assignment risk is actually sizing risk
- How smaller positions improve long-term survivability
- Why calm trading behavior comes from disciplined allocation
- How controlled scaling protects accounts over time

CHAPTER 18

KNOWING WHEN TO STEP ASIDE

One of the hardest lessons in income trading is recognizing that sometimes the best trade is no trade at all.

Stepping aside rarely feels productive. It can feel passive, cautious, or even indecisive. Yet professional trading is not defined by constant activity. It is defined by intelligent participation. Markets do not reward presence. They reward timing, discipline, and selectivity.

There are periods when markets simply do not compensate option sellers adequately for the risks required. Recognizing those moments and willingly holding cash becomes one of the most underrated skills in options trading.

Income strategies perform best when volatility is structured and price behavior remains rational. In those environments, probability behaves predictably and time decay works consistently. Premium reflects measurable risk.

But markets periodically lose structure. Earnings clusters, policy uncertainty, macro headlines, liquidity shocks, or rapid sentiment changes can create environments where premium expands while stability disappears. Prices move faster than adjustments can reasonably manage.

Premium may look attractive. Risk quietly becomes asymmetric.

Not all high implied volatility represents opportunity. Sometimes it signals instability.

Nugget: Not All Volatility Is Opportunity

High premium often exists because uncertainty is extreme.

1. When Participation Becomes Dangerous

The urge to act becomes strongest precisely when traders should slow down.

Income slows. Expirations pass without replacement trades. Cash levels rise. The psychological discomfort of inactivity begins building pressure.

Forced trades rarely begin recklessly. They begin subtly:

- choosing slightly closer strikes
- accepting weaker setups
- increasing size to compensate for fewer trades
- convincing yourself conditions are "probably fine"

Nothing appears dangerous at entry. Damage usually appears later, when adjustments become expensive, correlations rise, or assignment compounds exposure during unstable conditions.

Professionals recognize that bad environments punish otherwise good strategies.

Example: Choosing Patience Over Activity (NBIS)

A clear example occurred while managing NBIS. I held 500 shares while selling covered calls, but implied volatility gradually collapsed. Weekly premiums declined to levels that no longer justified downside risk or capital commitment.

The temptation was obvious: continue selling calls simply to maintain income flow. Instead, I allowed shares to be called away, accepted a controlled loss, and intentionally moved to cash. More importantly, I resisted redeploying capital immediately.

That pause restored flexibility. Emotional pressure declined almost instantly. Decision-making improved because capital was no longer trapped in marginal opportunity.

Weeks later, stronger setups appeared, allowing redeployment into positions producing significantly better premium and probability alignment.

The profit did not come from trading. It came from waiting.

Nugget: Cash Is a Position

Liquidity is active risk management.

Example: Stepping Aside During Portfolio Stress

During the 2026 technology volatility phase, multiple positions across both my Roth and individual accounts required active management simultaneously. HIMS remained in repair mode while RGTI, SOUN, and QUBT experienced rapid sentiment-driven swings.

At that moment, adding new trades would have increased complexity precisely when clarity was needed. Instead of layering additional exposure onto an already stressed portfolio, I reduced entries and allowed existing trades to stabilize.

Income slowed temporarily. Risk stabilized immediately.

That decision was not fear. It was allocation control.

Professionals understand that *portfolio attention is finite*. When existing positions demand focus, adding new exposure divides decision quality.

Sometimes defense means doing less.

2. The Psychological Resistance to Sitting Out

The greatest obstacle to stepping aside is psychological, not technical.

Income traders often feel obligated to produce weekly results. Inactivity creates discomfort that manifests as:

- boredom trades
- fear of missing rallies
- comparison to prior income weeks
- or pressure to maintain consistency

Activity feels productive. Selectivity is profitable.

Markets exploit impatience. Traders who feel compelled to participate become liquidity for those willing to wait.

Professionals redefine productivity. Waiting becomes work.

Nugget: Discipline Often Looks Like Inactivity

Doing nothing is sometimes the highest-skill decision available.

3. When Professionals Step Aside

Experienced traders intentionally reduce participation during environments such as:

- heavy earnings calendars
- macro-driven headline markets
- rapidly expanding volatility
- elevated sector correlation
- ongoing repair phases
- declining premium relative to risk
- emotional fatigue or decision overload

These pauses are temporary recalibrations, not abandonment of strategy. Stepping aside protects capital, restores emotional neutrality, and allows objective evaluation to return.

4. The Hidden Edge of Missed Trades

One of the most liberating realizations in trading is this: Missed opportunities rarely matter. Avoided disasters compound enormously.

Over a multi-year career, one missed winner changes little but one preventable drawdown changes everything.

Professionals measure success not by trades taken, but by damage avoided. Longevity is built quietly through restraint.

Nugget: Longevity Is the Edge

Survival creates opportunity repeatedly.

5. Stepping Aside as Active Management

Stepping aside is not retreat. It is a strategic pause designed to preserve decision quality and maintain optionality. Markets constantly cycle between opportunity and instability. Traders who remain fully deployed during every phase eventually encounter conditions that overwhelm flexibility.

Professionals participate selectively. They engage when probability aligns. They pause when structure deteriorates. They return when compensation improves.

Trading becomes sustainable when participation becomes intentional rather than habitual.

The goal is not constant income. The goal is uninterrupted survival.

In This Chapter, You Learned

- Why sometimes the best trade is no trade
- How unstable environments disguise risk as opportunity
- Why forced trades originate from income pressure
- How holding cash restores flexibility and clarity
- When stepping aside protects portfolio stability
- Why inactivity can be professional risk management
- How avoided losses compound more than captured gains
- Why selective participation creates long-term longevity

Part VI

REAL-WORLD RECOVERY CASE STUDIES

Up to this point, this book has focused on how professional traders think under pressure.

The preceding chapters explored volatility regimes, capital allocation, position sizing, emotional control, defensive adjustments, and the psychological realities that emerge when markets stop cooperating.

Now it is time to see what those principles look like inside real trades. This section shifts from framework to application.

What follows are not theoretical examples or reconstructed success stories. These are realistic recovery paths—the kind that unfold slowly when stocks decline unexpectedly, volatility expands, correlations rise, and multiple positions move red at the same time. Adjustments stretch across weeks or months. Progress appears uneven. Outcomes remain uncertain while decisions must still be made.

Part VI shows what durable trading actually looks like. Not the highlight reel. The grind.

What These Case Studies Are and Are Not

The examples that follow are methodical, probability-driven, and capital-focused. They demonstrate how exposure is managed when markets refuse to cooperate and when income trading becomes uncomfortable.

These are not:

- one-week recoveries

- aggressive comeback trades

- perfectly timed exits

- or hindsight-optimized decisions

There are no dramatic rescue moments.

Professional recovery is often slow, repetitive, and emotionally uneventful. That is precisely why it works.

If recovery feels urgent or dramatic, structure is usually being sacrificed. Durability is quiet.

Why You'll See Familiar Trades

Some tickers appear multiple times throughout this section, intentionally.

Real trading is not a sequence of isolated examples. Positions evolve across changing environments. The same trade may move from income generation, to defense, to repair, and eventually back to stability.

A stock reappears not because it was ideal but because it required management. These trades were not selected because they recovered quickly. They were selected because they demanded discipline over time.

That distinction reflects reality.

Professional trading is rarely about finding perfect trades. It is about managing imperfect ones well.

A Note on Real-Time Trading

Many positions discussed in this section were still active at the time of writing. Some remained in repair mode. Others were stabilizing gradually. A few outcomes were still unknown.

This is deliberate.

Professional trading rarely provides clean endings on schedule. Positions evolve across earnings cycles, volatility shifts, and sentiment changes. Decisions must be made without certainty about what comes next.

These case studies are presented as they actually occurred, unfinished, developing, and managed under live market conditions rather than reconstructed after outcomes were known.

The objective is not to demonstrate perfect results. It is to demonstrate professional decision-making while uncertainty still exists.

How to Read These Case Studies

As you move through this section, focus less on outcomes and more on process.

Pay attention to:

- Position size relative to total capital
- When adjustments were made, and when restraint was chosen

- How capital preservation guided decisions

- How delta and exposure were reduced over time

- Where patience replaced activity

- How structure improved before price recovered

Throughout each example, ask yourself one question: "Would I have reacted differently under pressure?"

That reflection alone will improve trading behavior more than any technical adjustment.

The Goal of Part VI

By the end of this section, you should:

- Understand what real recovery actually looks like

- Stop expecting fast fixes

- Recognize patience as a professional advantage

- See how probability reasserts itself over time

- Understand how survival precedes profitability

- Trust structure more than emotion

This section represents the transition from theory to survivability.

Because professional income trading is not defined by winning trades.

It is defined by trades that remain manageable long enough to recover.

CHAPTER 19

A HIGH-IV COLLAPSE REPAIRED

High-implied-volatility stocks attract income traders for an obvious reason: they pay exceptionally well. Premium appears abundant, income accumulates quickly, and trades often feel productive almost immediately after entry. Early success reinforces confidence, and participation begins to feel justified by results.

Yet the same volatility that produces attractive income also magnifies structural mistakes. High-IV environments rarely punish traders immediately. Instead, they reward activity long enough for exposure to build quietly beneath the surface. By the time risk becomes visible, positions are already established under assumptions formed in easier conditions.

This case study follows a real high-IV collapse using SOUN—not a catastrophic blowup, but something far more common and far more dangerous: a manageable trade placed under sustained psychological pressure. These are the trades that test discipline over weeks and months, where survival depends less on technical skill and more on behavioral restraint.

The objective throughout this trade was never perfection. The objective was control.

1. The Setup: Stacking Premium in a High-IV Environment

In October 2025, SOUN presented what many income traders actively search for: elevated implied volatility combined with strong liquidity and weekly option availability. Premium levels supported consistent income generation, and early trades behaved exactly as expected.

I began selling cash-secured puts across consecutive weeks:

- Oct 20, 2025: 15 contracts at $18.50 →$545.05 premium
- Oct 27, 2025: 15 contracts at $18.00 → $640.14 premium
- Nov 3, 2025: 15 contracts at $17.00 → $880.14 premium

Viewed individually, each position appeared disciplined. Strikes moved lower as price softened, deltas remained within acceptable probability ranges, and premium collection aligned with Wheel methodology.

Nothing looked reckless, and that was precisely the problem.

Each new entry increased directional exposure to the same underlying asset. Because income arrived consistently, concentration risk remained psychologically invisible. High-IV environments often disguise exposure buildup because positive feedback arrives faster than risk recognition.

Professional mistakes rarely feel dangerous when they begin.

2. Exposure Stacking—The Invisible Risk

The issue was not contract size alone. Assignment remained financially manageable, and portfolio allocation initially supported participation.

The true risk emerged from pacing.

Selling fifteen contracts once represents a position decision. Selling the same size repeatedly while price weakens gradually transforms participation into concentration. Exposure accumulates quietly because each individual decision appears reasonable at the time it is made.

High implied volatility does not merely test strike selection. It tests restraint.

Nugget: Monitor Risk

Premium arriving easily often means risk is building quietly.

3. The Collapse: Assignment and Psychological Pressure

Eventually SOUN continued trending lower and assignment occurred near the $17 strike. Assignment itself was expected. Within the Wheel framework, ownership represents transition, not failure.

The real challenge began afterward.

Price failed to stabilize. Instead of rebounding quickly, the stock drifted lower week after week. Premium declined alongside price movement, creating one of the most psychologically difficult environments for income traders:

- unrealized losses increased
- income declined simultaneously
- recovery appeared uncertain

This combination often triggers escalation behavior. Traders attempt faster recovery, tighter strikes, or larger trades elsewhere to compensate for slowing income.

Instead, objectives changed. Income was no longer the priority. Stability was.

Covered calls were introduced deliberately:

- Nov 10, 2025: $16 strike → $280.05 premium
- Nov 17, 2025: $14 strike → $125.05 premium

These trades were not designed to recover losses quickly. They were designed to slow deterioration while lowering cost basis incrementally.

Professional repair begins when urgency ends.

4. The IV Crush: When Opportunity Disappears

By December 2025, implied volatility contracted sharply. Weekly premiums collapsed into the $50–$60 range-levels insufficient to justify ongoing short-dated exposure.

At this stage many traders force activity simply to maintain income consistency.

I did the opposite. I stopped trading weekly. No forced entries. No marginal credits. No activity for activity's sake.

Stepping aside temporarily reduced income but restored flexibility. Capital remained intact, emotional pressure declined, and decision quality improved immediately.

Nugget: When the Market Stops Paying, Participation Becomes Risk

When option premiums collapse, forcing trades only increases exposure without meaningful compensation. Stepping aside protects capital until opportunity returns.

5. Structural Adjustment: Buying Time Instead of Speed

Rather than abandoning the position, duration was extended. Covered calls were moved two to four weeks out, allowing meaningful premium collection without introducing excessive assignment risk.

This adjustment accomplished several things simultaneously:

- reduced decision frequency
- increased premium efficiency
- lowered emotional noise
- allowed price stabilization time

Recovery did not accelerate, but control returned.

Professional recovery often looks slow precisely because it avoids introducing new risk.

6. Where the Trade Stands

As of early 2026, SOUN remains in managed repair. Adjusted cost basis has steadily declined while covered calls continue generating controlled income.

The trade is not finished, but it is survivable. And survivability, not speed, is the defining characteristic of professional trading.

Recovery in professional trading is measured by regained control, not by immediate profit.

7. What This Case Study Teaches

This trade demonstrates that high-IV failures rarely originate from a single decision. They emerge from cumulative exposure combined with delayed recognition of changing conditions.

Recovery required:

- accepting assignment calmly
- slowing participation
- extending duration
- abandoning income urgency
- allowing structure to improve gradually

High implied volatility rewards humility more than aggression.

In This Chapter, You Learned

- How exposure stacking develops quietly
- Why assignment is rarely the true danger point
- How IV collapse changes income expectations
- Why stepping aside restores control
- How extending duration stabilizes recovery
- Why survivability matters more than speed
- How disciplined pacing prevents escalation

CHAPTER 20

MULTI-MONTH WHEEL RECOVERY

Many traders imagine recovery as sudden. A strong bounce. A fortunate roll. One large premium cycle that erases discomfort.

Reality rarely works that way. True Wheel recoveries unfold slowly across months and through repetitive execution that often feels uneventful while it is happening. Progress becomes visible only in hindsight. During the process itself, improvement can feel frustratingly invisible.

This chapter documents what long-duration recovery actually looks like inside a live position.

1. The Beginning: Favorable Conditions

I began trading HIMS on July 7, 2025, during an environment supportive of income strategies. Liquidity was strong, implied volatility elevated, and premium levels justified conservative entries.

Cash-secured puts were layered gradually:

- July 7: 11 contracts at $42.50 → $718.70
- July 14: 21 contracts at $46.00 → $1,204.06
- July 21: 10 contracts at $47.50 → $563.36

- July 28: 12 contracts at \$54.00 → \$1,024.04

Each trade appeared rational independently. Deltas were acceptable, premiums attractive, and income consistency reinforced participation.

But exposure was growing faster than awareness. Layering positions during favorable sentiment created concentration risk that remained hidden while price cooperated.

Nugget: Premium Consistency Often Masks Growing Exposure

Steady income can quietly increase risk when positions accumulate faster than awareness.

2. The Turning Point

On August 1, 2025, negative media coverage shifted sentiment rapidly. Price declined sharply and assignment followed.

Assignment itself was expected. The problem was persistence. The stock did not stabilize. Declines continued. Headlines evolved. Market perception changed faster than recovery could occur.

At this moment many traders attempt escape, closing emotionally or forcing aggressive recovery trades. Instead, objectives shifted completely. Income stopped being the goal. Account stability became the goal.

3. Entering True Repair Mode

The position transitioned into structured recovery. Covered calls were sold consistently against assigned shares, not aggressively, but defensively.

Over six months, covered call premium totaled \$18,742.83.

Each sale served one purpose—lower cost basis slowly.

There was no dramatic solution. No single adjustment fixed the trade. Progress occurred through repetition applied under discipline. Some weeks produced strong premium. Others produced little. Some required doing nothing at all. Every week reduced pressure incrementally.

4. The Psychological Reality of Long Repairs

Extended repair phases challenge psychology more than strategy. Income slows, progress feels invisible, and uncertainty persists longer than expected. The greatest temptation becomes speed.

Speed introduces risk.

Throughout this period, I reduced new trades, lowered deltas, maintained higher cash reserves, and accepted slower portfolio income. These decisions protected flexibility while allowing probability time to reassert itself.

Professional recovery often feels uncomfortable precisely because it avoids dramatic action.

Nugget: The Grind Is the Edge

Professional income trading succeeds through disciplined repetition, not dramatic trades.

5. Six Months Later

As of early 2026:

- HIMS trades near $16
- Adjusted cost basis ≈ $34
- Position remains active
- No forced liquidation occurred

This represents my longest repair cycle.

Nothing heroic occurred. Only disciplined repetition. And that is the lesson most trading education ignores.

Recovery is not an event. It is a process.

6. What This Trade Proves

The Wheel Strategy does not promise avoidance of drawdowns. It provides a framework for surviving them.

Despite significant price decline:

- capital remains intact

- exposure remains controlled
- income continues
- flexibility remains available

Professional trading success is measured not by avoiding difficulty, but by preventing irreversible decisions during difficult periods.

7. The Truth About Multi-Month Recovery

Real recovery is slow. Repetitive. Emotionally demanding. Often unimpressive from the outside.

But durability compounds. The trader capable of managing six months of structured repair gains an advantage unavailable to traders seeking rapid outcomes.

Longevity, not brilliance, creates consistency.

Nugget: Longevity Is the Strategy

The traders who endure long repair cycles gain an advantage over those constantly chasing quick outcomes.

In This Chapter, You Learned

- Why multi-month recovery is normal
- How layered CSPs create hidden exposure
- Why assignment begins recovery—not failure
- How covered calls engineer cost basis improvement
- Why income slows during repair phases
- How patience restores structural control
- Why endurance defines professional trading

CHAPTER 21

WHEN CUTTING LOSSES WAS THE RIGHT CALL

Most trading books avoid this topic, not because it is rare but because it is uncomfortable. Professional option sellers do not advertise losses. They rarely highlight exits that lock in red numbers. Yet experienced traders understand an important truth: longevity in income trading does not come from avoiding losses entirely. It comes from recognizing when continuing a position no longer improves probability.

There are moments when rolling no longer restores structure, when time stops helping, and when repair quietly transforms into capital stagnation. In those moments, the professional decision is not adjustment or patience.

It is exit.

This chapter addresses one of the most misunderstood realities of income trading: sometimes survival requires walking away from a position that is still manageable—but no longer efficient.

1. The Dangerous Myth: "Time Always Fixes It"

Income strategies teach patience, and rightly so. Time decay, premium collection, and disciplined rolling often convert uncomfortable trades into profitable outcomes. Because this works frequently, traders begin believing time alone guarantees recovery.

Most of the time patience *does* work. Until it doesn't.

Time cannot repair structural deterioration. It cannot restore liquidity that disappears. It cannot recreate implied volatility once premium collapses. And it cannot compensate for capital trapped in positions that no longer justify attention or risk.

The Wheel Strategy is powerful. Rolling is powerful. Time is powerful. But none of them override poor capital efficiency.

Professionals understand that patience must remain conditional.

Nugget: Discipline Includes Knowing When to Quit

Holding forever is not strength. Holding blindly is weakness.

2. The Moment Professionals Reevaluate

Positions rarely become exit candidates overnight. The shift happens gradually. Premium declines. Adjustments stop improving structure. Management effort increases while reward decreases. Mental bandwidth becomes disproportionately consumed by a single trade.

At first, traders attempt minor fixes. Strikes are adjusted. Duration is extended. Expectations are lowered. None of these actions are wrong, but eventually a deeper question appears:

Is continued management improving my position, or merely delaying a decision?

Professional traders recognize this moment early. Amateurs often recognize it months later.

Example: NBIS—When Capital Needed to Move

I held 500 shares of NBIS while managing the position through covered calls. Initially, the trade behaved normally. Premium arrived consistently, and cost basis improved gradually through disciplined sales.

Then the environment changed.

Implied volatility contracted sharply. Weekly premium declined until calls generated minimal income relative to capital committed. The position required attention, monitoring, and ongoing management, but compensation for that effort continued shrinking.

Nothing catastrophic had occurred. The company had not collapsed. The shares had not imploded. The trade simply stopped functioning as an income engine.

Approximately $23,000 in capital remained tied to a position producing marginal return. At that point, the decision became mathematical rather than emotional.

I allowed the shares to be called away in the money and accepted a total realized loss of $678.30.

Small. Controlled. Intentional.

Nugget: A Small Loss Can Restore Large Opportunity

Sometimes you exit not because you failed, but because your capital deserves better deployment.

Example: When Repair Becomes Capital Drag

Another situation occurred during a lower-volatility phase within a technology holding where price stabilized but implied volatility compressed significantly. The stock stopped moving meaningfully, and premiums fell week after week.

Rolling remained possible. Covered calls remained available, but progress slowed to nearly zero. Each week produced activity without improvement.

This is one of the most deceptive scenarios in income trading. Nothing appears broken, yet capital quietly stops working. Traders often remain trapped because losses feel small enough to ignore.

Professionally, however, stagnation carries risk. Capital tied to low-productivity positions cannot participate when higher-probability opportunities appear elsewhere. Eventually, the opportunity cost exceeds the realized loss required to exit.

The professional decision is mobility.

3. Repair vs. Capital Efficiency

A critical distinction exists between positions that are temporarily red and those that have become capital inefficient.

Repairable trades typically show:

- stable fundamentals
- recoverable volatility
- meaningful premium opportunity
- improving structure over time

Capital-drag positions show something different:

- collapsing implied volatility
- minimal premium relative to capital
- prolonged stagnation
- increasing management effort without progress

Time helps the first category. Time often worsens the second.

Nugget: Time Cannot Fix Allocation Problems

Rolling adds time. It does not restore productivity.

4. Why Traders Refuse to Exit

The greatest resistance to cutting losses is rarely financial. It is psychological. Thoughts appear naturally:

- *I'll wait until break-even.*
- *I've already invested months managing this.*
- *It's only temporary.*
- *Selling now makes the loss real.*

These reactions are human. But professionals detach identity from positions. A trade is inventory, not validation.

Markets do not reward emotional endurance. They reward adaptive decision-making.

5. The Professional Exit Framework

Before exiting NBIS, several questions guided the decision:

- Has volatility remained supportive?
- Is rolling still improving probability?
- Is capital being compensated fairly?
- Does this position deserve continued allocation?
- Would I open this trade today?

That final question often provides clarity.

If the answer is no, continuation usually reflects attachment rather than logic.

Nugget: If You Wouldn't Enter It Today, Why Hold It?

Positions are tools, not commitments.

6. What Happened After the Exit

The most important part of professional exits happens afterward.

There was no revenge trade. No urgency to recover losses. No emotional repositioning.

Capital was redeployed deliberately into higher-IV opportunities where premium justified exposure. Stress declined immediately. Decision clarity improved. Portfolio flexibility returned.

The account continued functioning smoothly, not because losses were avoided, but because damage was contained early.

That is professional survival.

7. Cutting Losses as Risk Management

Professional income trading is not about winning every trade. It is about preventing irreversible outcomes.

A controlled loss preserves:

- capital mobility
- emotional stability

- opportunity access
- portfolio balance
- long-term income consistency

The trader who never exits eventually becomes trapped. The trader who exits strategically remains adaptable.

Nugget: Survival Is a Win

A controlled loss is not failure. It is tuition paid to stay in the game.

8. The Real Lesson

The objective of Volume II has never been perfection. It has been durability.

Sometimes durability means rolling. Sometimes it means assignment. Sometimes it means repair. And sometimes, the hardest decision of all, it means walking away calmly while the account remains intact.

Professional traders do not measure success trade by trade. They measure it by whether they are still operating years later.

In This Chapter, You Learned:

- Why time does not repair every position
- How capital inefficiency signals exit conditions
- The difference between repairable trades and capital drag
- Why ego delays necessary exits
- How opportunity cost justifies controlled losses
- The professional framework for cutting losses
- Why redeployment often outperforms persistence
- How survival sometimes requires stepping aside

CHAPTER 22

BECOMING A DURABLE INCOME TRADER

Most traders spend their careers trying to be right. Professional income traders spend their careers trying to last.

Volume II was never about maximizing returns but about maximizing survivability, because survivability is what ultimately produces returns. Income compounds only if the trader remains intact long enough for probability, time, and discipline to work together.

By this point, you have seen what real trading looks like under pressure. You have seen assignments that did not immediately recover, repairs that stretched across months, volatility regimes that changed without warning, and moments where the correct decision was not adjustment, but restraint or exit.

Durability is not theoretical. It is practiced.

This final chapter is not about strategy mechanics. It is about identity, because once identity changes, decisions follow automatically.

1. The Shift That Changes Everything

Amateurs focus on outcomes. They ask how much they can make this week, what the best trade is right now, or how quickly they can recover from a red position.

Professionals think differently. They ask:

- Can my portfolio withstand additional pressure?
- Am I sized to remain calm if conditions worsen?
- Will I still be trading confidently a year from now?

That difference appears small at first, yet it compounds more powerfully than any edge in strike selection or volatility timing. Over time, the trader who prioritizes survivability builds continuity, and continuity is the foundation of compounding income.

Nugget: Longevity Is the Edge

Markets don't reward brilliance once. They reward discipline over decades.

2. What Durable Traders Actually Do

Durable traders are not defined by perfect trades. They are defined by repeatable decisions made under uncertainty.

They roll when structure improves. They accept assignment when ownership lowers risk. They slow down during volatility expansion. They hold cash without guilt. They exit positions when capital efficiency disappears.

They understand something most traders learn too late: Success is rarely determined by the trades you win. It is determined by the damage you avoid.

3. Stability Over Speed

Durable traders are not obsessed with acceleration. They are obsessed with structure.

They accept that some recoveries require months. They allow income to fluctuate without abandoning discipline. They reduce size when uncertainty expands and step aside when markets stop compensating risk appropriately.

Speed increases fragility. Stability creates staying power.

A slow recovery that preserves capital will always outperform a fast recovery that introduces new exposure.

The objective is not weekly productivity. The objective is long-term operability.

Nugget: Survival Extends Opportunity

You only need average opportunities if you survive long enough to see many of them.

4. Income Is a Byproduct

One of the deepest lessons of this volume is simple: Income is not the goal. Income is the outcome.

When traders chase income directly, they tighten strikes, oversize positions, and force trades during unfavorable environments. When they instead protect capital, manage exposure, and maintain flexibility, income emerges naturally.

Income flows from structure. It disappears when urgency replaces discipline.

Nugget: Income Is Earned by What You Don't Do

Skipping a bad trade can be more profitable than entering a good one.

5. Identity Before Strategy

If you have absorbed the lessons of this book, you no longer think like someone chasing setups or predicting price direction.

You are becoming something different:

- a risk manager
- a capital allocator
- a probability operator
- a portfolio decision-maker

Your role is not to defeat the market. Your role is to remain functional inside it.

Once survival becomes the priority, emotional pressure declines. Decisions slow. Drawdowns become manageable rather than threatening. Confidence becomes quieter, but far more durable.

6. When the Market Tests You Again

And it will. There will be another volatility expansion. Another uncomfortable stretch where income slows. Another period where multiple positions move red simultaneously.

The difference now is not prediction. It is preparation.

You understand position sizing. You understand repair. You understand when patience helps, and when exit protects capital. You understand that unfinished recovery is still professional trading.

Discomfort no longer signals failure. It signals participation.

Nugget: Confidence Comes From Survival, Not Wins

Wins feel good. Survival builds belief.

7. The Quiet Advantage

Most traders study offense. They pursue entries, indicators, and strategies designed to produce rapid income. Few study defense.

You now understand defense:

- how drawdowns behave
- how emotion distorts decisions
- how to slow risk without freezing
- how to repair patiently
- how to redeploy capital intelligently
- how to protect longevity

This knowledge will not make trading exciting. It will make it sustainable, and sustainability builds wealth quietly.

8. Closing Reflection

Brilliance is loud. Durability is quiet.

Brilliance seeks validation. Durability builds continuity.

If there is one principle to carry forward from Volume II, it is this: The trader who survives the longest eventually wins.

Stay patient.

Stay appropriately sized.

Stay adaptable.

Stay disciplined.

Stay in the game.

Income is not built in weeks. It is built across years of controlled decisions made under pressure.

And now, you understand how professionals endure that pressure.

In This Chapter, You Learned:

- Why durability matters more than brilliance
- How professional traders prioritize survivability
- Why income follows structure rather than speed
- How identity shapes trading decisions
- Why defense creates long-term consistency
- How survival becomes a competitive advantage
- Why longevity, not perfection, defines success

VOLUME II GLOSSARY (A–Z)

THE DURABLE INCOME TRADER'S OPERATING MANUAL

This glossary reflects the defensive philosophy of *Selling Options for Income Volume II*. These are not academic definitions or textbook explanations. They are practical survival concepts shaped through drawdowns, volatility expansions, assignment cycles, and real recovery management.

A

Allocation Discipline: The deliberate limitation of capital exposure per position or sector to preserve flexibility during drawdowns. Proper allocation prevents temporary stress from becoming portfolio-level danger.

Assignment Acceptance: The intentional decision to take assignment rather than force a roll. A transition from obligation to ownership that often restores control when rolling no longer improves structure.

Adverse Move: A price movement against a position that increases unrealized loss or exposure. Normal in income trading and dangerous only when combined with poor sizing or emotional reaction.

B

Behavioral Risk: Risk created by fear, ego, urgency, revenge trading, or income pressure rather than market structure. Often the most expensive risk a trader faces.

C

Capital Drag: A position that consumes capital while producing insufficient premium or probability advantage. Not necessarily a bad trade, but an inefficient deployment of resources.

Capital Mobility: The ability to reallocate capital efficiently when a position no longer offers productive premium or acceptable probability. Trapped capital represents silent risk.

Capital Preservation: The primary objective of professional option sellers. Protecting capital ensures time and probability remain available to work.

Cost Basis Engineering: The deliberate, methodical reduction of effective share cost using time, premium collection, and disciplined covered call management. A process, not a shortcut.

D

Deep In-The-Money (Deep ITM): An option with substantial intrinsic value and minimal extrinsic value remaining. Requires structured management rather than hope-based decision-making.

Defensive Mindset: The professional identity shift from income chasing toward capital protection and survivability during uncertain market conditions.

Defensive Posture: A temporary shift toward reduced exposure, wider strikes, slower trade pacing, and increased cash reserves during unstable environments.

Defensive Rolling: Rolling an option to improve probability, extend duration, or reduce directional exposure—not to relieve emotional discomfort.

Delta Compression: The intentional reduction of directional exposure through wider strikes, extended duration, or reduced size. A method of lowering portfolio sensitivity without exiting positions.

Drawdown: A temporary decline in account value from a prior peak. Expected and survivable when allocation and discipline remain intact.

E

Emotional Urgency: The false sense of immediacy created by market movement that pressures traders into premature or unnecessary decisions.

Exit Discipline: The professional willingness to close or redeploy a position when probability, capital efficiency, or thesis quality deteriorates, even at a controlled loss.

Extrinsic Collapse: Rapid erosion of time value caused by deep ITM positioning or approaching expiration, reducing adjustment flexibility.

F

Forced Recovery: An aggressive attempt to repair losses quickly through oversizing, tight strikes, or probability abuse. Frequently compounds damage instead of resolving it.

G

Gradual Recovery: The professional approach to repairing positions through time, conservative premium collection, and incremental structural improvement rather than speed.

H

High-IV Environment: A market condition where elevated implied volatility increases premium while simultaneously magnifying directional and behavioral risk.

I

Income Mode vs. Recovery Mode: Two distinct operational states—*Income Mode* prioritizes consistent premium generation under stable conditions, and *Recovery Mode* prioritizes cost basis improvement, probability, and capital protection over income speed.

Irreversible Loss: Permanent capital damage caused by emotional decisions, oversizing, or rule abandonment rather than normal market movement.

L

Longevity: The defining advantage of professional income traders, the ability to remain solvent, rational, and active across multiple market cycles.

M

Market Stress: Periods of elevated volatility, correlation expansion, or macro uncertainty requiring defensive positioning and reduced exposure.

Mental Capital: A trader's psychological bandwidth. Emotional fatigue reduces decision quality as reliably as financial loss.

N

No-Volunteer Risk Principle: Refusing exposure during earnings events, major news catalysts, or unstable volatility conditions that do not offer favorable probability.

O

Opportunity Cost: The hidden cost of keeping capital tied to low-productivity positions instead of reallocating it toward stronger opportunities.

Oversizing: Allocating excessive capital to a single position, reducing flexibility and increasing emotional pressure.

P

Portfolio-Level Risk: Risk created when multiple positions move adversely at the same time, requiring system-wide management rather than individual trade decisions.

Portfolio Triage: The process of prioritizing adjustments when several positions are under pressure simultaneously. Not every position requires immediate action.

Probability Drift: The gradual deterioration of a trade's probability profile due to price movement or time passage, even when the original thesis remains intact.

R

Recovery Adjustment: A structured management action intended to improve position durability or probability—not an emotional reaction or new speculative trade.

Regime Transition: A market phase where volatility behavior changes faster than trader expectations adjust. Often the most dangerous environment for income strategies.

Rolling Under Pressure: Managing adjustments when options move deep ITM or volatility expands. Requires discipline, patience, and available capital.

S

Stepping Aside: The intentional decision to pause new trades when markets fail to compensate sellers adequately for risk. A strategic defensive action.

Strike Compression Repair: The gradual lowering of cost basis while carefully narrowing strike distance over time without increasing exposure aggressively.

Survival Mindset: The professional operating philosophy focused on remaining solvent, flexible, and emotionally controlled during market stress.

System Integrity: Maintaining trading rules and structure even when short-term outcomes are unfavorable.

T

Time Extension: Rolling or selecting longer-duration contracts to restore flexibility, rebuild extrinsic value, and reduce short-term decision pressure.

Time Leverage: The structural advantage option sellers possess when duration remains available. Time creates optionality.

Trading Identity: How a trader defines their role. Durable income traders operate as risk managers and capital allocators rather than speculators.

U

Unrealized Stress: Psychological pressure generated by open losses that have not produced realized capital damage but influence decision-making.

V

Volatility Regime: The prevailing market environment—calm, chaotic, or transitional—that determines position size, strike distance, and trading pace.

W

Wheel Repair Cycle: The disciplined process of using assignment and covered calls to gradually repair adverse entries while preserving capital and flexibility.

Z

Zero-Panic Rule: The nonnegotiable principle of never making major trading decisions during emotional spikes.

CLOSING NOTE ON VOLUME II

Volume II was never about making more trades. It was about learning how to survive when trades stop going your way.

Anyone can sell premium in calm markets. The real test begins when volatility expands, income slows, and discipline replaces comfort.

If Volume I taught you how to generate income, Volume II taught you how to defend it. And in the long run, the trader who survives difficult markets is the trader who remains in the game long enough for probability to work.

CLOSING REFLECTIONS

If you've made it this far, you've already done something most traders never do: you stayed.

You didn't search for shortcuts. You didn't chase the next shiny strategy. And you didn't assume discipline would somehow appear when markets became uncomfortable. Instead, you chose to understand what truly separates traders who endure from those who quietly disappear.

You've learned that drawdowns are not failures of skill, but tests of structure. You've seen that volatility is not an enemy to fear, but an environment to manage. Most importantly, you've learned that survival in the markets is not passive, it is deliberate, intentional, and earned through disciplined decisions made under pressure.

The case studies you've just seen were examples of durable decision-making unfolding in real time, often without certainty or clean endings. That is where professional traders are actually formed, not during easy wins but during uncomfortable periods that demand patience instead of reaction.

Most traders fail because they lack durability. They trade too large, expect perfection, and panic when stress inevitably arrives. This book exists because income trading is not about avoiding discomfort. It is about absorbing pressure without breaking your system, or yourself.

There will still be red weeks. There will still be uncomfortable positions. There will still be moments when patience feels harder than action. The difference now is perspective. You understand how to slow down instead of speed up, how to think instead of react, and how to protect capital instead of chasing recovery.

You are no longer trying to win every trade. You are building longevity.

Durable traders do not rely on brilliance, perfect timing, or constant excitement. They rely on time, discipline, probability, and emotional control. Those who survive long enough allow compounding to accomplish what force never can.

If Volume I taught you how to generate income and Volume II taught you how to defend that income, the next step becomes clear—learning how to scale it without increasing fragility.

That is the purpose of Volume III, which will focus on building a more advanced income engine-scaling strategies, portfolio structuring, diversification across underlyings and durations, and higher-level management systems designed to maintain consistency across changing market environments.

Keep learning. Keep refining. Keep building durability.

Trading mastery is not achieved through a single strategy or a single book. It develops through repetition, experience, and steady improvement across changing market environments.

If you found value in *Selling Options for Income Volume II*, there are two simple ways to continue building alongside this series:

1. Leave a Review

Reviews help other traders discover disciplined, risk-focused education instead of hype-driven shortcuts. Even a short, honest review makes a meaningful difference.

2. Continue With the Series

Each volume builds intentionally on the last:

- **Volume I** – Building consistent income using the Wheel Strategy
- **Volume II** – Managing risk, drawdowns, and long-term survivability
- **Volume III** – Scaling income intelligently across portfolios and market regimes

The goal has never been fast profits. The goal is longevity.

Thank you for investing your time, discipline, and trust in this work.

Tony Perez

ACKNOWLEDGMENTS

This book was shaped by real trading experience, not only during profitable stretches but during drawdowns, uncertainty, frustration, and the discipline required to remain consistent when markets stopped cooperating. The lessons in these pages were earned through experience, patience, and many moments that tested both strategy and mindset.

To my family, thank you for your patience, understanding, and constant support. Trading and writing both demand long hours of focus and reflection, and your encouragement makes that commitment possible.

To fellow traders and friends, thank you for the honest conversations, especially the ones centered on mistakes, recovery, and discipline during difficult markets. Those discussions, often shared during challenging periods rather than successful ones, influenced this book more than you may realize.

To the readers, thank you for choosing depth over shortcuts. Volume II was written for traders willing to look beyond excitement and focus instead on resilience, clarity, and longevity. If this book helps you remain calm during drawdowns, protect capital under pressure, and stay disciplined when emotions run high, then it has fulfilled its purpose.

And finally, to the markets, relentless, humbling, unpredictable, and endlessly instructive, thank you for teaching lessons that no textbook ever could. Every setback carried insight, and every challenge reinforced the truth that durability matters more than brilliance.

FEBRUARY 4, 2026
NYSE OPENING BELL®
NEW YORK STOCK EXCHANGE
C LISTED
C LISTED
NEW YORK STOCK EXCHANGE

ABOUT THE AUTHOR

Tony Perez is a multifaceted creator, trader, and storyteller whose work bridges financial strategy and military action fiction. As a self-taught trader, Tony is known for breaking down complex concepts into simple, actionable steps anyone can understand.

He emphasizes discipline over prediction and consistency over excitement, principles that form the backbone of this guide.

Tony is also the author of the James Chase military thriller series:

- *The Delta Mission*
- *The Dragon and the Eagle*
- *Cuba Libre*

Whether writing about battlefield strategy or financial strategy, Tony brings the same commitment: make it real, make it clear, and make it useful.

He lives in Florida, where he continues to trade, write, and help others build financial and personal freedom one mission and one premium at a time.